THE 4X4 BLOCK SCHEDULE

J. Allen Queen
Kimberly G. Isenhour

EYE ON EDUCATION
6 Depot Way West, Suite 106
Larchmont, N.Y. 10538

Library of Congress Cataloging-in-Publication Data

Queen, J. Allen.
    The 4 x 4 block schedule / by J. Allen Queen and Kimberly Gaskey
Isenhour.
        p.   cm.
    Includes bibliographical references.
    ISBN 1-883001-56-0
    1. Block scheduling (Education)--United States.   I. Gaskey
Isenhour, Kimberly.   II. Title.   III. Title: Four x four block
schedule.   IV. Title: Four by four block schedule.
LB3032.2.Q84   1998
371.2'42--DC21   98-10667
                                                            CIP

Production services provided by:
Bookwrights
1211 Courtland Drive
Raleigh, NC 27604

ACKNOWLEDGMENTS

We would like to express our appreciation to our families for their love and tolerance. We would also like to thank Nan VanHoy, Mary Shelton Drum, and Dana Wrights for their insights, ideas and experience. Additionally, we would like to express our gratitude to Robert Sickles and the staff at Eye on Education for their guidance and support.

We dedicate this book to Dr. Martin A. Eaddy, Superintendent of Lincoln County Schools, North Carolina. We appreciate his early vision of the 4x4 block and the opportunity to work with the faculty, staff and students in all of his high schools over an extended period of four years.

PREFACE

After reading pages of research and making numerous visits to schools using an alternative schedule, many educators return to their schools eager to implement a form of block scheduling. With this decision, they will be faced with an exciting challenge that will serve as a catalyst for educational reform into the next century. Block scheduling provides students with a unique educational opportunity and educators with a truly relevant framework to begin the reconceptualization of curriculum and instruction. Educators will find that block scheduling may be used as a catalyst for change. It is more than just an administrative tool, it can become the basis of a belief system designed to deal with an onslaught of problems. The possibilities for positive and meaningful change are real with block scheduling if educators implement a well developed program.

This book is designed to provide several elements for the successful transition from a traditional scheduling model to a 4x4 block scheduling model. Educators interested in the 4x4, semester, or accelerated scheduling model can use this text as a complete guide in the design and implementation for each step in the transitional process.

From years of the authors' research, teaching and daily involvement with blocked schools, educators can expect certain trends to occur after the first semester, the first year and then subsequent years. First-year teachers can benefit from the text as well as preservice teachers who are completing state teaching licensure. This text may be used by schools on a 4x4 block schedule that need to revitalize their program or move into the next phase of scheduling.

Block scheduling can become a dynamic framework to create a safe school and a productive learning environment. Fewer class changes and a reduction in discipline referrals help to create a school environment which is calm and inviting. The reduction in the student/teacher ratio promotes a warm and nurturing classroom climate as teachers have time to address the individual needs of students. Block scheduling will positively impact climate and the increasing rate of discipline problems in schools.

The move to a new schedule or the revitalization of an old schedule provides educators with the chance to establish a common vision for schooling, one where there is unconditional positive regard for students and the teaching of an internal locus of control. Students learn to make positive choices and take personal responsibility from teachers and the community.

Our text is the only comprehensive text on the topic of 4x4 block scheduling. *The 4x4 Block Schedule* is a detailed step-by-step practical guide for educators to learn the processes of curriculum alignment and how to design and use pacing guides. The book concludes with numerous examples of instructional strategies that have been modified for the 4x4 block schedule model. Also included are ready to use letters, procedures and guidelines for working with teachers, parents and students.

The book is divided into three parts. Part I includes Chapter One which is an introduction to the 4x4 model. Part II is composed of smaller chapters (Chapters Two through Eight) where we focus on the basic stages and steps used in designing the 4x4 block model. The procedures and models for implementation are presented in Part III in Chapters Nine and Ten.

ABOUT THE AUTHORS

Dr. J. Allen Queen is a former classroom teacher and school principal. He is presently a professor in the Department of Middle, Secondary and K–12 Education at the University of North Carolina at Charlotte, NC. He is the author of several books and numerous professional articles in the field of education. Allen has conducted seminars and workshops all over the United States in block scheduling and classroom management. He completed his undergraduate and graduate work at Western Carolina University and took his doctorate at The University of Virginia. He resides in Kings Mountain, North Carolina with his wife Patsy and his son, Alex.

Kimberly Gaskey Isenhour taught English for several years at Maiden High School during the transition between a traditional schedule to a 4x4 block schedule. Currently, she is teaching Communication Skills at Mt. Pleasant Middle School and collecting research on making a successful transition from middle school to a blocked high school. She has traveled extensively teaching 4x4 seminars and has served as a consultant to school systems moving to a block schedule. She has authored several professional articles in the field of education. Kimberly received her undergraduate and graduate degrees from the University of North Carolina at Charlotte and plans to pursue a doctorate. She resides in Concord, North Carolina with her husband Chris.

TABLE OF CONTENTS

PART 1

INTRODUCTION

1

Using Time More Effectively: Why Block Scheduling?

In the past decade, business, industry and government leaders have proposed methods for improving the American public school system. The media have scrutinized practically every suggestion or program developed for school renewal. Their combined voices continue to reiterate the obvious need to reform education on a national scale and the fear inherent in failing to do so. The launch of Sputnik in 1957 became a symbol of American failure and served as a catalyst for educational reform. No longer could Americans lazily believe that their system of education was producing the top students in the world. Students in the United States were in jeopardy of falling far behind foreign students if reforms were not immediately implemented. President Eisenhower established the Commission on National Goals in the late 1950s, which was followed by numerous committees, conferences, and reports on the state of education in the United States.

The bombardment of reports on the inefficiency of schools continued to produce alarm over the lack of student preparation for the workplace. In 1983, *A Nation at Risk* was published under the auspices of Terrel Bell, then Secretary of Education, appointed by Ronald Reagan. The report revealed the poor condition of American schools and posed many questions about the effectiveness of the current concept of schooling. Bell formed the National Commission on Excellence in Education to examine the current educational system, report findings of quality, and make suggestions for improvement. The resultant report, *A Nation at Risk*, documented the closing academic gap between American children and children from other industrialized nations and the alarming rate at which foreign students were surpassing American students.

In response, educational organizations, business groups, university commissions, and various interest groups created documents of reform recommendations. Many of these recommendations included a section on lengthening the amount of time students spend in a learning environment. The Carnegie Council on Adolescent Development emphasized the need for concentrated time blocks of learning in its report, *Turning Points: Preparing American Youth for the 21st Century.* "Students need time to learn and teachers should be able to create blocks of time for instruction that best meets the needs of the students, responds to curriculum priorities and capitalizes on learning opportunities such as current events" (1989, p.52). Recently, The National Education Commission on Time and Learning (1994) proposed that the academic day be doubled, that the school day be reclaimed for instruction, and that schools be reinvented around learning, not the scheduling of time.

In the 1996 NASSP annual convention, a report of the NASSP study of the restructuring of the American high school was presented in partnership with the Carnegie Foundation for the Advancement of Teaching. *Breaking Ranks: Changing an American Institution* listed nine goals with priorities for renewal in the areas of curriculum, instructional strategies, school environment, technology, organization and time, and assessment and accountability. The NASSP report also established a desirable web of support which included working toward professional development for teachers and principals, understanding and respecting diversity, streamlining of governance, providing resources, seeking ties to higher education, and actively reaching out to form relationships with the community. Finally, to ensure successful school renewal, the report called for strong leadership.

With the great influx of recommendations and sets of priorities, schools may find it confusing to determine a set path for school-level renewal. It is not one single plan or program that can be implemented to solve all ills; it may be that schools must adopt a philosophy of change or develop an ability to adapt to the future. Of interest to reformers, the management of time has been seen as a tool used by the administration in moving students through the day. With the institution of block scheduling, time can become more than a mere tool. A blocked schedule or flexible schedule can be molded to fit the needs of any school's instructional, physical building, climate, student management, accountability, assessment, and fiscal considerations.

Time alone is not the only concern educators have in developing a successful schedule; a continual search for the best way to meet the needs of every student remains a primary focus. Because of this quest, many schools have adopted numerous programs with varying levels of success. The hasty adoption of a program often leads to a quick fix syndrome where the new program serves as a simple cover for underlying problems. Also, the quick fix program may not be accepted by the faculty and staff, who should be the driving force behind implementation of any new idea. Block scheduling or any other program is not easily implemented in a school system unless a majority of the school staff adopts the ideas behind the new concept. The rapid acceptance of block scheduling as a viable reform effort is in large part the result of several key factors: the call for an increase in credit hours for graduation, the call for increased ability to take electives, the prevention of teaching limitations experienced in short choppy classes, the desire to create a personal educational environment, and the impetus to reduce discipline problems often caused by constant class changes. Block scheduling provides choices and various alternative means to address these key factors in schools today.

A BRIEF HISTORY

National, state, and local agencies have continued to question the quality of education in schools with respect to the effective use of time. These questions often include the search for the use of time, the allocation of time, and the ability to account for time. Short-term solutions for the time allocation issue are usually rooted in past recommendations. These solutions were intended to create more time for learning by lengthening the school day and year, instead of pushing for the efficient use of the existing school time. Utilizing flexible scheduling and avoiding the mere lengthening of the total hours spent in school are less costly and more realistic in solving the time allocation problems.

Analyzing time can be simplified by classifying the various types found in a typical school schedule. In examining the nature of time, designations can be made of the usage of the time in a given school day. Divisions of time are made in the total amount of time available in a school day, the time designated for instruction, the time allocated for academic subjects, the time in which students are engaged in a learning activity, and the academic learning time in which students experience high rates of success. The goal of school renewal with regard to time is to increase the academic learning time to directly correlate with student achievement (Murphy, 1992).

Traditional scheduling fits the industrial mind-set of educating the masses in a cost-efficient and timely manner. Inflexible scheduling serves the constraints of the general institutional needs, but does not match the pedagogical practices proven to meet the needs of individual students.

The flexible modular plan or the Trump Plan was designed by J. Lloyd Trump in 1959. The focus of the Trump Plan was to eliminate the rigid high school schedule and institute classes of varying lengths depending on the learning needs of students. A science class could meet for a 40-minute lecture, a 100-minute lab and a 120-minute help-session per week. Still other classes may have only met for a "module" of 20 minutes. Teachers were encouraged to utilize a variety of instructional formats to teach large groups of over 100 students down to small groups and individual study (Trump, 1959). Despite this innovative organization of time and the initial program excitement, flexible modular scheduling failed because of problems relating to student discipline and the general movement and organization of students throughout the day. Students were given as much as 40 percent of the day for individual learning, which resulted in a lack of structure and severe discipline problems. Teachers also complained about the difficulty in changing teaching practices to fit the flexible lengths of time (Goldman, 1983).

The block scheduling of today had its infancy in several forms throughout the United States. Many schools in the 1980s experimented with language arts and economics/civics blocked classes, where they simply combined two of the single periods into one 110-minute class. This combining of classes was not new, as vocational schools throughout the United States had used double periods and extensions of time for decades. Slowly, schools adopted entire schedules with blocked classes and began to adjust teaching styles and strategies to better meet student needs. The 4x4 block scheduling model, A/B block scheduling model, and the Copernican Plan were instituted with varying degrees of success.

THE PROCESS OF SCHOOL RENEWAL

Renewal with regard to scheduling is highly organic and changeable as there are many types of scheduling solutions that meet a wide range of school, teacher, and student needs. As previously stated, before the institution of blocked classes, schedules were generally organized with six to eight daily periods of instruction. The length of these periods ranged from 45 to 55 minutes with 3 to 5 minutes for changing classes. Graduation requirements in most states have been steadily increasing, which allows little opportunity for electives. In an attempt to offer vocational, art, and other elective opportunities, the class time decreased and the school day became even more disjointed and chaotic (Canady & Rettig, 1995).

Today, these short instructional periods contribute to a negative school climate with teachers battling to cover the curriculum. The course content, not the students' learning needs, becomes the teachers' focus. Students are also overwhelmed by six to eight different teachers, several sets of class rules, multiple homework assignments, stacks of books, and an overload of exams. Carroll describes the typical day for a high school student as consisting of "seven different classes, a homeroom, and a cafeteria 'nine different locations' in a six and one half-hour day. In addition, if they have physical education, these young people may change clothes twice and shower once. This is not a schedule that fosters deep reflection" (1990). The high school students' fragmented day does not often make a cohesive whole as, "The subjects come at a student . . . in random order, a kaleidoscope of words: algebraic formulae to poetry to French verbs to Ping-Pong to the War of the Spanish Succession, all before lunch" (Sizer, 1992). Students accumulate fragments of information and are tested on how well they can memorize details and facts. High school students are encouraged to participate in athletics, music programs, dramatic productions, and other extracurricular club activities that require as much as two hours of time after school. Many students also have part-time jobs to help support the ownership of an automobile or their own families. Students are working a frenzied 12-hour day with little time to relate their high school education with past experiences or attain individual focus on special interests they may have in any given subject (Carroll, 1990, p. 365). High school, therefore, may be seen by many as a set of tasks that must simply be endured and "real life" will follow after graduation. Students are pushed to the contemporary rite of passage 'graduation' with no real world skills, or ability to problem-solve. This is also the trend in higher education.

Not only do the students languish in the six to seven period days, teachers are limited to the types of instructional strategies they can use in shortened periods. Lecture is the most efficient way to expose students to a large amount of information in a short time frame. Highly effective teaching strategies such as Paideia seminars (Adler & Van Doren, 1984), cooperative learning, synectics, concept attainment, inquiry methods, role-playing, case methods, and simulations are difficult to implement in a span of 20 to 35 minutes (Canady & Rettig, 1995). The 6 to 8-period days also promote isolation of teachers from one another and compartmentalization of knowledge rather than its integration. Teachers are unable to get to know their students as individuals and a great deal of their daily energy is spent monitoring student movement through halls up to eight or nine times a day, recording attendance in as many as eight classes, and recording grades for 150 or more students (Miller, 1992). As the student population increases in diversity, teachers must struggle to meet the emotional and academic needs of heterogeneous classes in which they may not have time for accurate assessment.

COMPARING THE BLOCK SCHEDULING MODELS

In general, there are several current organizations of block scheduling. These organizations are divided into the 4x4 Block Schedule; the A/B Block Schedule; a Copernican, Modified Block or Macroschedule (Carroll, 1990).

STRUCTURE OF THE 4X4 BLOCK SCHEDULE MODEL

Classes in the 4x4 model of block scheduling are taught in longer periods of approximately 90 minutes and meet for only a part of the school year, usually one semester. (See Example 1.) The 4x4 model has also been called the **semester schedule** or an **accelerated schedule** as only four courses are taught per semester. Students have the opportunity to take eight different classes in one academic year. Teachers teach three classes per semester and use the fourth period of their day for planning. "Educators have always been concerned about having enough time to complete the course content. Because of that, they found themselves looking for ways to change the traditional six- or seven-period day" (Queen, Algozzine, & Eaddy, 1997).

Unlike the A/B schedule (discussed later), the 4x4 further limits the focus of students to four classes per semester so there are fewer homework assignments, quizzes, and tests. This allows for concentration on new topics and time for mastery. Students also have the opportunity to repeat failed classes within the same year and still graduate on time, which is an incentive to remain in school. Where applicable, many students opt for advanced study on and off campus as greater freedom is possible within the 4x4 schedule. Vocational departments in schools using a 4x4 schedule experience a resurgence in the number of students enrolled in courses and in the demand for new courses on a yearly basis. For teachers, the 4x4 schedule reduces the preparation to three classes of between 50 to 90 students. However, planning must now involve more than preparing the usual

---

EXAMPLE 1. SAMPLE 4X4 SCHEDULE

First Semester	Second Semester
Course 1 First Period (90 Min.)	*Course 5* First Period (90 Min.)
Course 2 Second Period (90 Min.)	*Course 6* Second Period (90 Min.)
LUNCH	LUNCH
Course 3 Third Period (90 Min.)	*Course 7* Third Period (90 Min.)
Course 4 Fourth Period (90 Min.)	*Course 8* Fourth Period (90 Min.)

lecture. Various strategies that meet individual learning styles, alternative assessment and integration of content may now be planned for students. Lunch periods in smaller schools have sometimes been reduced to a single 45-minute period that serves for club meetings, teachers' office hours, detention, transfer student remediation, and general remediation.

The 4x4 scheduling model does, however, raise questions as to the ability of students to retain information over long periods of time that may occur between courses. It is possible for a student to finish Algebra I in the fall of his or her ninth grade year and then take the next math class in the spring of the tenth grade year. While it is advisable to take sequential building courses as closely together as possible, teachers on the 4x4 have not noticed any great difference between students who recently finished a prerequisite course and students who finished the building course some time earlier. Carroll reported no "consistent significant differences" between the retention of Copernican students and traditional students (1994). Students on the

4x4 schedule must have a balanced work load of difficult and elective courses each semester. One semester should not be full of electives while the other overloaded with difficult academic courses.

STRUCTURE OF THE A/B BLOCK SCHEDULE MODEL

Alternative day schedules or A/B block schedules alternate periods within the day or week. The classes usually meet every other day for extended blocks of time or a combination of alternating blocks and shortened classes taught every day for the entire year. Other modifications may be made to the A/B model by doubling a blocked class so that "A" days are Monday and Tuesday, followed by "B" days on Wednesday and Thursday. Fridays are rotated each week between "A" and "B" courses. (See Example 2.) Problems may arise with the A/B schedule as the course load for students is not focused on four courses at a time, the students are enrolled in eight courses for an entire year. Many students have also expressed confusion as to whether a day is "A" or "B."

EXAMPLE 2. SAMPLE A/B SCHEDULE

"A" Day Monday	"B" Day Tuesday	"A" Day Wednesday	"B" Day Thursday	"A" Day Friday	"B" Day Monday
Course 1 (90 Min.)	Course 5 (90 Min.)	Course 1 (90 Min.)	Course 5 (90 Min.)	Course 1 (90 Min.)	Course 5 (90 Min.)
Course 2 (90 Min.)	Course 6 (90 Min.)	Course 2 (90 Min.)	Course 6 (90 Min.)	Course 2 (90 Min.)	Course 6 (90 Min.)
LUNCH	LUNCH	LUNCH	LUNCH	LUNCH	LUNCH
Course 3 (90 Min.)	Course 7 (90 Min.)	Course 3 (90 Min.)	Course 7 (90 Min.)	Course 3 (90 Min.)	Course 7 (90 Min.)
Course 4 (90 Min.)	Course 8 (90 Min.)	Course 4 (90 Min.)	Course 8 (90 Min.)	Course 4 (90 Min.)	Course 8 (90 Min.)

STRUCTURE OF THE COPERNICAN PLAN, MODIFIED BLOCK, OR MACROSCHEDULING MODELS

The Copernican Plan, the modified block, or macroscheduling models arrange classes of differing lengths in several plans (Carroll, 1990). The modified block offers students the opportunity of taking classes of over 200 minutes in length, classes of 110 to 90 minutes in length, and classes of traditional length. Carroll predicted the following advantages of the Copernican Plan: "Virtually every high school in the nation can decrease its average size by twenty percent; increase its course offering or number of sections by twenty percent; reduce the total number of students with whom a teacher works each day by sixty to eighty percent; provide students with regularly scheduled seminars dealing with complex issues; establish a flexible, productive instructional environment that allows effective mastery learning as well as other practices recommended by research; get students to master twenty-five to thirty percent more information in addition to what they learn in the seminars and do all of this within approximately present levels of funding" (Carroll, 1990).

In 1994, Carroll reported his findings from a study of eight high schools that utilized the Copernican Plan. His findings included improved student attendance, a decrease in suspensions, reductions in dropout rates, greater content mastery seen in higher grades and credits earned, and a favorable rating for the Copernican Plan as opposed to the traditional schedule. With these approaches becoming more available, educators began moving to the block.

WHY GO TO THE 4X4 BLOCK?

Teachers and principals saw the advantages of moving to the 4x4 block schedule. A few of these are listed below:

Block scheduling may:

1. Cut the number of class changes and movements that large groups of students make in one day;

2. Reduce the number of administrative tasks performed in one day by teachers and students;

3. Improve the student-teacher ratio so that teachers can know more about each student's individual learning and social needs;

4. Help teachers make effective use of planning time by reducing the number of different courses taught in one day;

5. Promote in-depth study through cooperative learning, individual projects and labs that last longer than one day;

6. Promote the use of various teaching strategies and hands-on learning;

7. Match learning time to the learner and to the course content;

8. Reorganize the traditional department structure to promote an integrated curriculum.

THE SUCCESS OF THE 4X4 BLOCK SCHEDULE MODEL

The authors view the 4x4 block scheduling model as the best model for today's high schools. It is worth noting that teachers have developed what may be considered a philosophy which goes beyond the basic perimeters of the administrative aspects of mere scheduling and assigning students to classes. To support this philosophical ideal, educators also view that using a variety of instructional strategies has brought about a sense of reform within the secondary school. Therefore, we will focus the remaining part of this text on the 4x4 block scheduling model. The reader should be forewarned of the authors' obvious bias and the belief systems that have developed around this new philosophy and reform effort found in the successful implementation of the 4x4 block.

Blocked classes in the 4x4, A/B, or other modified schedules offer teachers and students many advantages. The lengthened classes increase the amount of instructional time because teachers spend less time on procedures, routines, and directions. There are only three to four starts and stops as compared to the six to eight reviews and closures of the traditional schedule. The

4x4 schedule offers a greater amount of quality instructional time than the A/B schedule because less time is spent reviewing. Teachers and students using the A/B schedule must review material covered two days prior (Canady & Rettig, 1995).

The blocked classes also provide time for extended lessons with a greater continuity. Science teachers may better plan and set up for labs and classroom experiments. English teachers can guide students through the entire writing process in one period and provide time for editing peer workshops. More guided practice and time for skill enhancement is provided for music, art, and vocational classes. Field trips to locations close to the school may be taken in one period or over lunch and a period.

The number of times students change classes is reduced and the discipline problems associated with changing classes, such as tardies and other inappropriate actions, are dramatically reduced. The hallways in schools are quieter and cleaner. Since the students are not in the hallways, vandalism of the school property also decreases (Canady and Rettig, 1995).

Teachers and students are initially concerned about maintaining interest in a longer class period. The traditional lecture and discussion model of teaching used in the past does not work well if it is overused in the block classes. There is a place for lecture and discussion if it is incorporated with a variety of other teaching strategies which meet the instructional needs of individual students. The added time allows for differentiated lessons to be designed and lessons that maintain high interest. The use of alternate models of instruction, such as cooperative learning, inquiry, group discussion, concept development, role-playing, exploration of feeling, conflict resolution, Paideia seminars, and synectics, is possible (Gunter, Estes, & Schwab, 1990). In a recent three-year longitudinal study conducted by the authors, teachers rated the 4x4 block. (See Graphs 1, 2, 3 and 4.)

Students enjoy the concentrated time spent studying fewer subjects. Further, students on a 4x4 block schedule have only four classes a semester to concentrate on, instead of the eight classes the traditional or A/B block schedules require. Teachers benefit from intensive planning time for only three classes. Less changes, fewer students, and less topic changes enable teachers to spend less time on daily administrative tasks and gives them

GRAPH 1. DOES INSTRUCTIONAL TIME IMPROVE BECAUSE OF THE 4X4 SCHEDULE?

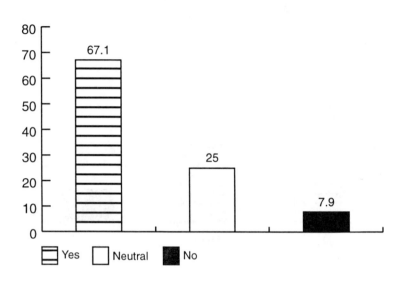

GRAPH 2. DOES THE INSTRUCTIONAL PACING OF COURSES IMPROVE BECAUSE OF THE 4X4 SCHEDULE?

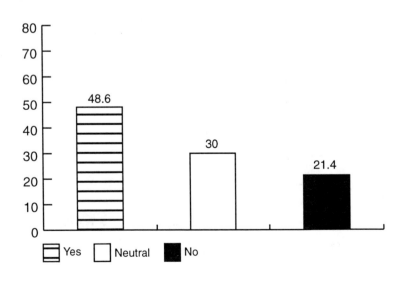

GRAPH 3. DO YOU FEEL THAT THE OVERALL RATING OF THE 4X4 IS SUPERIOR, AVERAGE OR UNACCEPTABLE?

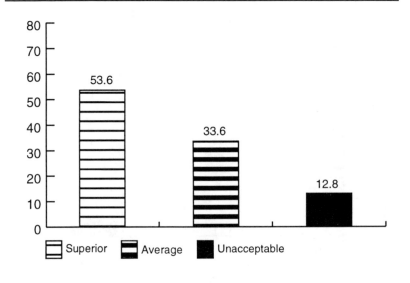

GRAPH 4. DID THE 4X4 SCHEDULE ENABLE YOU TO VARY YOUR TEACHING METHODS?

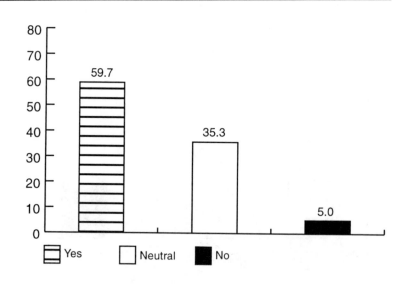

added opportunity for instructional planning time. Some teachers, depending on the subject taught and the school size, will still have three different preparations, but the majority of teachers do not have this type of load.

When students miss class, they have fewer teachers to see about missed work. Obviously, students will miss more content from a blocked class than a traditional class. It is imperative to establish homework policies to complete missed assignments. However, if students fail to complete the missed work, they will have the option of repeating the course.

Students are given another chance to remain with their age-mates if they fail a class in the 4x4 block. Should a student fail a class during the fall semester, he or she can retake the class during the spring or fall of the following year. This second chance limits the need for summer school and helps students to maintain a high self-esteem. There is a higher probability for students to remain in school if they can keep pace with their age-mates and graduate on time. In serious discipline situations, the principal can suspend a student for a semester instead of an entire year in the 4x4 block without placing the student a full year behind. On the opposite end of the continuum, the 4x4 can be advantageous to the high-achieving student.

Not only do students have chances for repeating courses or receiving remedial help, they have opportunities for acceleration. When students are not able to take algebra in the eighth grade, the traditional schedule does not permit the student to progress to calculus by the senior year. Additionally, students in a 4x4 block schedule can take two foreign language classes in one year and may be able to complete the equivalent of five or more years of a language before graduation. Other options for acceleration include independent studies, opportunities to take higher levels of math, and courses from local community colleges and universities.

Students are able to accelerate the level of the academic core courses that they complete and are able to take a greater number of electives than students in a traditional schedule. It is possible for students to earn up to 32 credits by the end of their high school career. As a result of this possibility, graduation requirements are steadily increasing in schools that utilize block

scheduling. Students who normally took only college prepara-
tory classes have the ability to take vocational, art, and physical
education courses, or in some situations, more advanced core
courses. In the author's three year, longitudinal study of 4x4
schools in North Carolina, teachers reported that the 4x4 caused
an increase in student achievement. (See Graph 5.)

Even though schools are offering more courses, it is possible to reduce some expenditures. Fewer textbooks are needed
and the money saved can be redirected to purchase instructional
materials needed to meet the needs of a variety of learners. Half
of the students required to take a particular course do so in the
fall semester and the same set of books can be reused in the
spring.

Block scheduling has been criticized for several reasons, such
as the loss of retention from one level of a course to the next, the
requirements of too much independent study needed outside
of class, the fitting in of transfer students who arrive from schools
not on a block schedule, the limited number of new electives
offered, college admissions, and the continued overuse of lecture in the classrooms. Yet, all of these criticisms may be solved
with appropriate plans of action and proper teacher training.

Students in a blocked schedule could possibly take a foreign
language class the first semester of their freshman year and then
not take the second language class until the spring semester of
their sophomore year or later. As stated earlier, it is imperative
that sequential or building classes be offered as closely together
as possible for obvious retention reasons. However, many
schools on the block do not report this as a major problem
(Canady & Rettig, 1995). Researchers have discovered that retention is affected by the original learning. The better students
learned the material in the first place, the better they will retain
the material. Retention for facts is always lower than retention
for comprehension and skills. However, this is true in any scheduling design. Other retention issues arise with AP classes. Students may take a blocked AP class in the fall and are not able to
take the AP test until the spring. These students may not be far
enough through the course in the spring to successfully complete the test which is given in early May. This issue is being
addressed with the testing companies to give the tests in Janu-

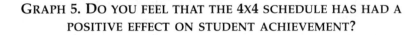

GRAPH 5. DO YOU FEEL THAT THE 4X4 SCHEDULE HAS HAD A
POSITIVE EFFECT ON STUDENT ACHIEVEMENT?

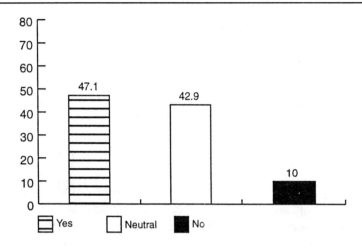

ary and June. The authors have encouraged numerous school systems to begin the fall semester earlier so exams and end-of-course tests can be given prior to the holidays.

Transfer students become problematic in the 4x4 semester plan when they arrive from schools that are on another schedule. To deal with these students, administrators often require the transfers to drop their core academic courses if they arrive in the fall semester. These core classes would then be resumed by that student in the spring. When students arrive in the spring, they may enroll in the core classes where they will more than likely receive a review along with new material. There is still much controversy over the issue of student transfer and incorporation in the 4x4 block.

IMPROVED CLIMATE

Due to the opportunities provided by block scheduling, individual students are able to experience a wide variety of positive innovations. The positive change in school climate is a result of the reduction in class size, the increase in subjects offered, and the ability of students to study new material in a hands-on, concentrated manner. The ability to flex schedules to meet the needs of an increasingly diverse population is a reality in the block scheduling program. In one county surveyed by the authors, teachers and students reported a positive change in school discipline as a result of the 4x4 schedule. (See Graph 6.)

The selection of a block schedule requires close analysis of the needs of the students, teachers, administrators, the school, and the community. The benefits of molding the schedule to meet the school or school system relates to ownership of the model. When a school community can select an appropriate model, the ownership and responsibility inherent in their choice create a sense of unity. If a particular schedule is forced on a school community, it may never be accepted and will usually fail.

The addition of electives such as astronomy, mythology, technical writing, aerobics, computer programming, advertising, and foreign language classes past the first two years gives students exciting choices. On surveys, students have consistently responded in a positive manner to the addition of electives, and this is further indicated by increased enrollment in these classes. The possibilities for students to take a wider range of vocational, art, and higher-level core classes energizes school communities to see the future of their schedule. As noted, apprenticeships, mentor programs, and post-secondary study in local community colleges are easy to accommodate in the lengthened periods. Remedial classes can be offered to students who have transferred from a school on a traditional schedule or to students who need extra attention in a specific course. When the curriculum is aligned to incorporate the required core courses with meaningful electives, the climate continues to improve.

The climate in the school and classroom is also positive when teachers move away from the *introduction - lecture - review* format and vary the presentation of content. If the class structure changes every 20 to 30 minutes, interest can be maintained. An experiential-based classroom full of cooperative learning, critical thinking, process writing, and active learning will keep the pace brisk and the students engaged in learning. Teachers and students are often surprised by the positive change in the classroom climate as the atmosphere is charged with energy and activity. Finding ways of organizing student movement for

GRAPH 6. DO YOU FEEL THAT THE 4X4 SCHEDULE HAS HAD A
POSITIVE OR NEGATIVE EFFECT ON SCHOOL DISCIPLINE?

Students   Teachers

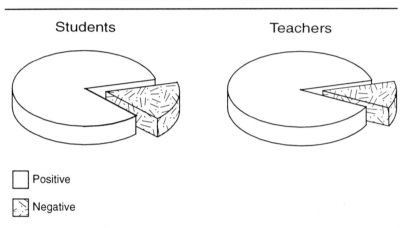

☐ Positive

▨ Negative

stimulus variation will give relief from sitting for extended periods. This movement should take place daily and can be accomplished by simply moving to a group activity or by retrieving
individual portfolios for additions.

Evidence of improved school climate can best be seen in the
decrease of reported discipline problems and in the cleanliness
reports from the custodial staff. Students move around the school
fewer times throughout the day, which produces a safer and
less frenzied atmosphere that can be significant for motivation
and student management. The pace of the school day is slowed,
while active learning and interaction between teachers and students are increased. This increased pace in the classroom may
cause fatigue during the first semester for both teachers and
students simply because the schedule is new. If careful attention is given to the balance of students' and teachers' schedules,
this fatigue will quickly subside. Once the first semester is over,
the second semester begins with a sense of renewal and what is
equivalent to a new school year. Students return after winter
holidays ready for new classes, teachers, and experiences.

By varying instruction, teachers area able to reach students
from diverse backgrounds and learning styles. Methods such
as cooperative learning increase positive social attitudes about

self, school, and peers, and can be used to foster open-mindedness and appreciation for others. Projects must require interdependence, individual responsibilities, and specified goals. Along with varied teaching methods, teachers are also able to assess students in alternative ways. This assessment may be in the form of portfolio presentations, group and individual project grades, surveys, products, computer-designed models/presentations, and oral reports.

By assessing the opinions through surveys, the school community can continue to have a voice in the schedule. This voice empowers students and creates a focused and excited group of learners. The school climate is affected by the continual efforts of addressing individual needs of students and the chance for teachers to be creative within the blocks of extended time. Schools have surveyed their communities and found that most parents and students like the new schedules and would never want to return to a traditional schedule. Likewise, some principals have surveyed or informally interviewed teachers and found similar results. The change is worth any initial struggles because the block schedule excites school communities about the possibilities of the future and the capability of educators to differentiate instruction (Queen & Gaskey, 1997).

RESEARCH REPORT

One county in North Carolina with three distinct high schools each having a population of 750 to 900 students, was observed by the authors over a period of four years. Prior to moving to the block schedule, each School Improvement Committee was asked to make site visits to 4x4 schools and report findings to their faculties. The county decided to adopt the 4x4 schedule and developed a strong staff development plan to implement the new blocks of time. The training program that was created by a selected committee and university advisors focused on preparing teachers in preparing pacing guides which were aligned with the North Carolina Standard Course of Study. The training also focused on developing skills with interactive instructional strategies that met the needs of various types of learners. After the initial summer training, follow-up activities were necessary to assist teachers in their delivery of instruction in the new block schedule format. The university advisors ventured into many classrooms throughout the county to observe teachers on a weekly basis. From these observations, constructive criticism and suggestions for follow-up training were delivered on a continuous basis.

After the first year, questionnaires were distributed to teachers, students, and parents. Each survey contained similar items and focused on the effectiveness of the 4x4 model. Teachers were observed by administrators using the state teacher performance instrument, and these observations were used to plan training sessions in specific instructional strategies. Teachers who experienced difficulties teaching in the blocked classes were required to develop and implement a professional improvement plan.

From observations, interviews, surveys, and state yearly performance data, perceptions of the overall success of the 4x4 model were analyzed over a four-year period. Researchers found that 70–80 percent of teachers, students, and parents believed the program was successful and desired to continue using the schedule in future years. The program had the strong support of school administrators, central office staff, and the superintendent. The research also revealed that teachers were using a variety of strategies, yet there was still an overuse of lecture in at least 30 percent of classes. Teachers reported an ability to spend 70 percent of their instructional time in interactive instruction with students and less than 15 percent of their time managing discipline problems.

Improvements were immediately evident as test scores rose after the first semester on a blocked schedule. The gains were maintained at a higher rate in social studies than in any other area tested. After examining scores over three consecutive years, the trend seems to be for higher scores after the first semester with scores declining after the second semester in each year. This is consistent with other schools that have similar experiences. The yearly averages are showing improvement, but the improvement would be greater if the level of achievement could be sustained through the second semester. A reason for first semester success over the second semester could be the excitement of a new year after summer break when students and teachers are energized. Fatigue may develop near the end of the second semester or lower performing students may be enrolled in the state-measured end-of-course tests during the second semester.

In another recent study (Queen & Gaskey, 1997), teachers responded to a survey which rated the teachers' perceptions of scheduling effectiveness. Eighty-four percent of teachers on a 4x4 block schedule felt that they were better able to vary instructional methods as a result of the schedule. Of teachers on a traditional schedule, only 44 percent felt that the schedule enabled them to utilize various instructional strategies. Seventy-nine percent of the teachers on a 4x4 reported an increase in the number of electives offered to students and 84 percent of teachers noted that the fewer class changes resulted in a safer school environment. Administrators using a 4x4 block schedule were asked the same questions and interestingly, 94 percent of administrators felt that the schedule gave their teachers the ability to better meet the needs of individual students and 81 percent of administrators saw an improvement in the school climate. Administrators reported the continued need for teacher training and for creative solutions to handling transfer students. Overall, 81 percent of teachers and 100 percent of administrators who were surveyed felt positively about the success of the 4x4 block scheduling model and its implementation in their schools. Only 60 percent of teachers and 55 percent of administrators using a traditional schedule reported feeling positive about their current schedule.

In a separate study of students in two school systems that included twelve high schools, respondents were asked to rate student discipline in the 4x4 block. After one year on the block, 51 percent of students indicated that school discipline had improved over the previous year; in fact, 18 percent indicated that behavior had improved substantially. No change in behavior was observed by 22 percent of students, and only 8 percent indicated that there was a decrease in the quality of student behavior.

A 4x4 School Is a Safe School

Schools that were originally designed to educate the traditional student must now adapt the curriculum and the instructional program to the needs of an increasingly diverse student population that has lower tolerance levels for ineffective teachers and traditional approaches to learning. Block scheduling may be one approach that gives students greater choices in course selections and gives teachers an extended time period to use a variety of interactive instructional techniques. Block scheduling helps to create an ideal setting to improve the learning environment.

Due to the opportunities provided by block scheduling, individual students are able to experience a wide variety of positive innovations. The positive change in school climate is a result of the reduction in class size, the increase in subjects offered, and the ability of students to study new material in an interactive, concentrated manner. The ability to flex schedules to meet the needs of an increasingly diverse population is a reality in the block scheduling program (Queen & Gaskey, 1997).

The climate in the school and classroom is also positive when teachers move away from the introduction - lecture - review format and vary the presentation of materials. If the class structure changes every 20 to 30 minutes, interest can be maintained. An experiential-based classroom full of cooperative learning, critical thinking, process writing, and active learning will keep the pace brisk and the students involved in learning. Teachers and students are often surprised by the positive change in the classroom climate as the atmosphere is charged with energy and activity. Finding ways of organizing student movement to give relief from sitting for extended periods and to help students stay focused can be accomplished by simply moving to a group activity or retrieving portfolios.

Evidence of improved school climate can best be seen in the decrease of reported discipline problems and in the cleanliness reports from the custodial staff. Students move around the school fewer times, which serves to produce a less frenzied atmosphere.

Block scheduling has been used in different formats in schools for decades. Secondary principals and teachers working in the secondary school should be aware that block scheduling has returned to the school with great support by educators, students and parents involved with the model. In fact, the 4x4 model especially has gained great support and is viewed by many educators as a philosophy within a new reform movement. Well-crafted schedules facilitate the use of time, space, and other resources, improve school climates, and provide solutions to a variety of problems related to delivering instruction. The 4x4 design is one of the many alternative structures for scheduling classes that is used in the secondary schools today. With respect to discipline, the authors found when comparing three schools in a local school system, discipline problems had decreased dramatically after the first year. In two of the schools, discipline referrals to the office were decreased by over 35 percent. In one school using Queen's *Responsible Classroom Management for Responsible Students and Teachers* and the 4x4 block model, office referrals decreased almost 70 percent after the first year. Queen (1997) found that one school that used the block and a responsibility-based schoolwide discipline plan had consistently improved discipline by more than 40 percent as measured by office referrals and school suspensions.

REFERENCES

Adler, M. & Van Doren, C. (1984). The conduct of seminar. *The Paideia Program: An Educational Syllabus.* New York: Macmillan, pp. 15–31.

Canady, R.L. & Rettig, M.D. (1995). *Block scheduling: A catalyst for change in high schools.* Princeton, NJ: Eye on Education, Inc.

Carnegie Council on Adolescent Development (1989, June). Turning points: Preparing American youth for the 21st century. Carnegie Corporation of New York, p. 52.

Carroll, J.M. (1987). The Copernican Plan: A concept paper for restructuring high schools. Paper presented at the Annual Meeting of the American Association of School Administrators, New Orleans, LA.

Carroll, J.M. (1990, January). The Copernican Plan: Restructuring the American high school. *Phi Delta Kappan, 72,* pp. 358–365.

Carroll, J.M. (1994, October). The Copernican Plan evaluated: The evolution of a revolution. *Phi Delta Kappan,* pp. 105–113.

Evaluation brief - Blocked scheduled high school achievement: Comparison of 1995 end-of-course test scores for blocked and non-blocked high schools. (1996). North Carolina Department of Public Schools.

Goldman, J.J. (1983). Flexible modular scheduling: Results of evaluations in its second decade. *Urban Education,* 18(2), pp. 191–228.

Gunter, M.A., Estes, T., & Schwab, J. (1990). *Instruction: A models approach.* Boston: Allyn & Bacon.

Miller E. (1992). Breaking the tyranny of the schedule. *The Harvard Education Letter,* pp. 6–8.

Murphy, J. (1992, March). Strategies for principals, instructional leadership: Focus on time to learn. *NASSP,* pp. 19–25.

National Commission on Excellence in Education (1983). *A nation at risk: The imperative for educational reform,* Washington DC: U.S. Government Printing Office.

National Education Commission on Time and Learning (1994). Prisoners of time: Report of the National Education Commission on Time and Learning. Washington, DC: U.S. Government Printing Office.

National Association of Secondary School Principals 1996 Conference Report. Breaking ranks: Changing an American Institution. Presented in partnership with the Carnegie Foundation for the Advancement of Teaching.

Queen, J.A., Algozzine, B. & Eaddy, M. (1997). The road we traveled: Scheduling in the 4X4 block. *NASSP Bulletin,* 81(588), pp. 88–99.

Queen, J.A., Algozzine, B. & Eaddy, M. (1996). The Success of 4X4 Block Scheduling in the Social Studies. *The Social Studies,* pp. 249–253.

Queen, J.A., & Gaskey, K.A. (1997, October). Steps for improving school climate in block scheduling. *Phi Delta Kappan,* pp. 158–61.

Sizer, T.R. (1992). *Horace's compromise: The dilemma of the american high school.* Boston: Houghton Mifflin.

U.S. Department of Education. (1983). *A Nation At-Risk: The Imperatives of Educational Reform*. National Commission on Excellence in Education. Washington, DC: U.S. Government Printing Office.

U.S. Department of Education. (1994). *Goals 2000: Educate America Act*. Washington, DC: U.S. Government Printing Office.

Trump, J.L. (1959). Images of the future: A new approach to the secondary school. Washington, DC: *National Association of Secondary Principals*.

PART 2

STAGES IN DESIGNING THE 4X4 BLOCK SCHEDULE

2

THE FACULTY:
THE FIRST STAGE IN
IMPLEMENTING THE
4X4 BLOCK SCHEDULE

STEP ONE: MOTIVATING THE FACULTY

For schools on a traditional schedule that are planning to look at alternative scheduling models, the first task is to examine the possible use of a block scheduling model. School administrators can take this first step by taking a poll or informal survey during a faculty meeting. Along with the survey, a simple discussion of present school needs can elicit the level of interest in transitioning to a block scheduling model. We have found that many teachers and members of the community have misconceptions about the block, therefore it is imperative to begin research on scheduling methods and have solid answers for any inquiries. From numerous workshops, teachers usually list the following as perceived strengths and weaknesses of 4x4 block scheduling:

Perceived strengths of 4x4 block scheduling:

◆ Get to know students better.

◆ Time for projects, research, and videos.

◆ Time to complete activities in one period.

◆ Students have fewer subjects to prepare for.

◆ Fewer papers to grade.

◆ Leads to the integration of curriculum.

◆ Takes learning to an application level.

◆ Discipline.

◆ Better use of facilities.

◆ Improved planning among faculty.

◆ Less time for students to be in the hall.

◆ Opportunity to practice effective teaching strategies.

◆ Students feel less rushed.

◆ Time for review, teaching, and practice.

◆ Time for administrative procedures like taking roll.

◆ Flexible schedule provides opportunities for remediation.

◆ Acceleration of learning.

◆ Opportunity to earn more credits.

◆ Students have fewer teachers and therefore less opportunity for conflict.

◆ Better variety of electives.

◆ Exploration of more subject areas.

◆ Longer engaged instructional time which leads to less stopping and starting.

◆ Fewer textbooks needed.

Perceived weaknesses of block scheduling:

◆ Lack of knowledge, information and training in the initial implementation.

- Class time is too long.
- Transfer students.
- Holding students' attention.
- Teachers not changing their teaching strategies.
- Gaps between sequential courses.
- The way students make up loss of class time.
- Determining the appropriateness of the 4x4 for our school by finding research to support any decision.
- Covering the material for exit exams and making sure there is time to teach the course content.
- Fear of change by students and teachers.
- Loss of total class time.
- Faster pace leaves some students behind.
- Less time for clubs and extracurricular activities.

In addition, teachers expressed a degree of concern in making a change to the block for these reasons. The main reason seems to stem from the simple fear of change itself. Prior to inservice training and a genuine effort by the administration to include teachers in the change process, teachers have often listed the following fears and concerns about moving to any form of block scheduling:

Initial fears and concerns:

- Club participation will suffer.
- Time gaps in subject areas.
- No community support.
- Inability to use time wisely.
- Transfer students from nonblocked schools.
- Absenteeism and problems with make up work.
- More electives class offerings will result in a need for more teachers, but not hired.
- Fear of improper implementation.

♦ Student graduating early.

♦ Will it last or is it a fad?

♦ Preparation time will increase dramatically.

♦ Student retention of material will be less.

♦ Overloading students with two concepts in math each day may be too much.

♦ Living through the end of the year twice.

For these typical fears and misconceptions to be allayed, it is imperative for the administration to include the faculty in the process of transition. Also, it is our recommendation that only forward progress can be made if at least 50 percent of the faculty are willing to begin the process of examining the use of block scheduling. Once the faculty have been presented with the idea of block scheduling in their school, three things should occur. The first is the selection of a design team, a curriculum committee, or an organized group composed of teacher representatives and one administrator. The second task is to read current literature and research available about block scheduling and discuss these findings within the committee. To complete the third task, teachers will have to visit many schools using the block. Committee members should visit schools that have been successful and unsuccessful in implementing the block model and investigate the reasons why schools on the block are successful or not successful. After detailed analysis of all the findings, the committee members present these to the faculty with the recommendation to accept or reject a particular block design.

STEP TWO: ROLE OF THE ADMINISTRATION

The next step of the process includes defining the role of the administration. Administrators will present the initial concept of the block model; however, it is highly effective to have innovative teachers who are eager to move toward futuristic models and take active leadership roles. The committee of these motivated teachers would work under the direction of supportive administrators and be involved in presenting the majority of the initial information to the faculty. After the presentation has been made, teachers will evaluate the information, collect their own data and seek answers personally from committee members. The committee should seek consensus of teachers who are interested in adopting the proposed model. If a large majority of teachers favor the move, it is worth initiating the next phase known as the implementation stage. To reach consensus, leaders attempt to bring out the supportive aspects of the program and try to resolve any of the negative aspects through negotiation. Items that are negotiated should include major elements considered barriers to consensus. In reaching consensus, the faculty does not vote, but gives a general statement of support to experiment with the new program. A word of caution is offered here about the dangers of voting. Voting often divides the faculty, usually over minor conflicts of negative attributes of block scheduling. The administration and the committee must try to encourage consensus first. However, if a consensus is not reached, and it is evident that a large percentage of the faculty is in support of change, then the authors recommend a secret ballot vote. From our work with numerous schools, we found that if at least 70 percent of teachers are eager to adopt some type of block scheduling model, the program has a greater possibility for success. Teachers voting against a schedule change may be planning to retire soon or may view any change as negative. It will become quite obvious which teachers disfavor the block. Often, these teachers may either retire or seek a transfer instead of going through the change process. In some cases, administrators will be able to help speed up this process. Negative attitudes of dissenting teachers only serve to sabotage the program. Once the faculty has decided to move forward, it should be agreed upon that the new model will be implemented within the next year or two.

STEP THREE: FACULTY ACCEPTANCE OF THE 4X4

In the unfortunate event that the administration requires a unilateral move to the block or fails to seek faculty support, teachers may feel undervalued, angry, and adversarial. Resenting the change, teachers will not benefit from the philosophy of block scheduling as a reform tool. We suggest that administrators or faculty leaders meet with faculty members individually or in small informal groups. Again, we have experienced that if principals choose teachers with futuristic beliefs, they can serve as change agents who search for school improvements. These types of teachers will be quite evident and can be selected informally by the administration The question guiding the newly identified leadership team should be, for example, "How can we help gain teacher support for the 4x4 model?" Top teachers need to be asked, "How can you help us gain teacher support for the 4x4 model?" We have used questionnaires to assess the feelings of faculty involved in the change process.

When principals and assistant principals allow teacher committees to take leadership roles, the administration gives the teachers ownership of the new model. The administration guides the transition, assists the teacher committee, and provides resources for the faculty during the change process. Teachers who have been identified as being resistant to the change would benefit from speaking with a well-respected teacher who could appeal to their willingness to be team players and contribute to the change. Many times, allaying fears that teachers have about their feelings of insecurity or about making a fast move can be accomplished by reassuring teachers that the change process will occur in a slow and orderly fashion. Teachers will need the constant reassurance of the administration and the committee that their hesitancy is understood and that their fears will be addressed. Many of the teachers may retain a degree of wariness of the unknown. This is usually mild and will subside with periods of success. In more severe cases, teachers who have major reservations but have agreed to make the change must be given special attention and greater reassurance.

3

INSTRUCTION:
THE SECOND STAGE IN
IMPLEMENTING THE
4X4 BLOCK MODEL

STEP ONE: CURRICULUM ALIGNMENT

Curriculum is perhaps the most disagreed upon term in educational literature, but it is perhaps the most important in that it serves to give educators the direction for what is to be taught in schools. *Curriculum,* which comes from a Latin term means to run a course. Curriculum definitions within the educational community define it in a more functional manner. Definitions center upon purpose, objectives, and organization of content. Historically, Hilda Taba (1962) viewed curriculum as a plan for learning and that all curricula,

> "... no matter what the design, are composed of certain elements. A curriculum usually contains a statement of aims and of specific objectives; it indicates some selection and organization of content; ..." (p. 10).

Many curricularists view curriculum to be product-oriented, i.e. specific outcomes, blueprints for instruction, or a plan for instruction. Other curricularists believe curriculum to be more process oriented to include instruction. Many educators view curriculum and instruction as being the same. **We believe curriculum to be the specific standards, goals and objectives which have been designed as the intended outcomes for learners.**

Definitions tend to have a philosophical flavor and vary greatly. Choosing a curriculum design has always been controversial. Of the several different approaches to designing curricula many are diametrically opposed.

The authors believe that most state and school systems use several different levels for curriculum development progressing broad, general goals to specific, behavioral instructional objectives.

In addition to new, varied instructional strategies and methods of assessment, overall curriculum organization must be addressed during staff development to ensure the success of block scheduling implementation. Teachers moving to the block must be able to "re-examine the curriculum and redefine priorities regarding what is to be covered in courses and how to pace a course within the new time structure" (Rettig and Canady, 1996). The ability to re-organize and reexamine what is most important in a course is vital since about ten percent of actual time in the classroom is lost in the block schedule. Reid (1995) says that "block schedule works for teacher who are able to reconceptualize the curriculum. They do not just past two former lesson plans together into one longer one." Two suggestions that Wyatt (1996) has to assist teachers in reconceptualizing the curriculum are curriculum mapping and curriculum integration. Wyatt says that curriculum maps are useful in allotting time efficiently in the block. She states that teachers should "map their content delivery, working backwards by semester, quarter, month, week, and finally by day." She also says that with the extended class period, more guided practice time should be utilized.

Curriculum integration is a result of effective curricular mapping. Teachers can gather in grade-level groups with their individual curriculum maps and "brainstorm some logical connections that could support and strengthen the instruction across content areas" (Wyatt, 1996). We have found similar data. Teachers had to redesign their courses for a 90-day period as compared to the traditional 180 days, requiring the development of pacing guides and the restructuring of traditional units and lesson plans. In fact we found instructional pacing as the top skill for success in the block as noted through observation, survey data, and teacher interviews. Teachers should receive training on how to restructure their currently used pacing guides for the longer class period and shortened calendar of the block schedule.

Curriculum alignment is a first step towards being successful in using the 4x4 block schedule. From our work with teachers, if this element is not reviewed by teachers it will negatively impact the amount of content that can be covered in a specific time period. The first three elements in curriculum alignment from our perspective are scope, sequence, and scheduling. **Scope** tends to be related to the amount of content in the curriculum and what is to be taught in a certain period of time. Educators develop a K–12 perspective curriculum from viewing scope as the basic outcome of what students are to learn in the formal schooling process. In finalizing the program structure, one may examine math, writing, or science programs for specific outcomes related to subject area. In the scope, the teacher can see what is to be taught in specific courses.

In sequencing, teachers must examine the order of instruction to be taught for achieving specified standards or objectives. Teachers strive to put content in a meaningful order. Some courses such as mathematics and science are sequential and require a step-by-step approach. In process skills such as observing, comparing, and inferring, there may be a definite order in which higher-order process skills are developed. In the sequencing, evident patterns emerge at various levels in the high school. In high school courses, the sequencing becomes extremely important in order to include all of the desired content. Most of the content has been prescribed by the various state departments and the local boards of education. In most states, teachers will find biology being taught in the tenth grade; however, in other places it may be taught in the eleventh or the ninth grade. In any case, the scope of the content is similar. To be educationally sound, the sequence should be that basic biology is taught be-

fore advanced biology and usually before chemistry and physics courses. Once courses have been developed for scope and
sequence, scheduling is the next step.

The process where administrators and curriculum leaders
get involved is at this stage. Their role is to make sure that course
offerings are presented at a particular time and offered on a regular basis to ensure all students the opportunity to take the classes.
Scheduling becomes more important as we move from curriculum alignment to instructional alignment in that if the courses
are not aligned in the schedule in the right fashion, it will be
difficult to implement the desired curriculum.

To realign the curriculum, teachers can use one or more of
our three basic models that realign the curriculum in a manner
that allows for the maximum use of time and desired content.
This is called the ABC-D Plan. (See step-by-step description in
chapter 9.)

STEP TWO: INSTRUCTIONAL PACING GUIDES

Instructional pacing can determine whether a teacher successfully completes the course, unit or lesson in that the guide
helps the teacher to remain on schedule. Additionally, student
attention and effective use of time in 90-minute classes can be
major concerns to educators. Fear of losing learning time and
student attention may be a concern for some teachers but longer
class time may be the answer for students to learn better. Teachers must be able to effectively facilitate the classroom in order
for the students to keep on task and for instruction to flow
smoothly. Therefore, the development of appropriate pacing
guides is essential.

Statistical research on attention capability and time on task
within the block scheduling realm has been extremely limited.
There are recommendations that pertain to these issues, but most
data concerning block scheduling and students' attention are
located within specific programs to account for addressing these
issues. Due to this fact, little actual teacher or student information exists through clinical studies, but concern about this issue
is addressed in block programs from the beginning.

Educators and researchers have identified the many positive aspects that block classes have on student attention and

time on task. Fitzgerald (1996) said, "The major power of longer teaching periods is that such periods make attention to brain-compatible teaching principles far more feasible." (p. 20). Brain-compatible teaching deals with the attempt of teachers to maximize the attention span and information retention of students. The "idea is to cycle between focused or concentrated activities and more diffuse or relaxing activities as a natural pattern for the brain." He believes that this can be increased if school staff members are equipped with advanced training in using time efficiently and effectively to meet students' brain-compatible learning needs (Fitzgerald, 1996, p. 21).

Another positive aspect of longer classes, is the ability for teachers to be able to spend more time with students who do not learn at the same rate or the same way as most of their other students do. This would allow students to be able to excel in subject areas that they would have not otherwise. With larger periods of time, teachers can also use other forms of instructional strategies such as, discussion, group work, multimedia presentations, and student research projects to diversify the class and let students do more independent work for grades instead of just lecture, review, and test. This ability for instructional diversity adds for better attention on behalf of the students because with several different activities within a class period, constant attention on one activity does not occur.

With longer instructional time, teachers who formally taught within the traditional program, may have had a hard time adjusting to longer class time. Hackmann and Schmitt (1997) said that a typical reaction may be, "What in the world am I going to do for that many minutes?" (p. 1). During their first year in block scheduling, many teachers tried teaching two lessons in one period. They were not provided with the needed guidance, instruction, or support to be able to teach effectively within the longer classes. One teacher commented, "We didn't know anything, really, about block scheduling, and it would have been nice to have other teachers, not administrators, college professors, folks from the state department of education, or consultants tell us what to expect." (Jones, 1995, p. 19).

One attention related issue concerning block scheduling, concerns the relevance of presented subjects and lessons. To keep students following the lesson, it is necessary to relate the lesson to something they can see relevance. If a teachers is teaching a lesson concerning the some element of the Civil War, a link to identifying with that period is needed. By using a modern life occurrence or strategy, the students are better able to mentally comprehend the lesson at hand. The negative issue is that most teachers in blocks as well as those who are not, do not keep students' attention through relevance. Mastery learning and significant memory retention also suffer from not connecting the past with the future.

The issue of attention and the effects that longer block classes have on attention has been a question for educators as they enter into the block scheduling program. The ideas and concepts of longer time periods are generally positive. We have found this to be true in the 4x4 model, especially when teachers see effective instructional strategies. Effective teachers can incorporate oral presentation, technology, discussion, research projects, and other collaborative activities into the longer lesson for greater success.

According to Hackmann and Schmitt (1997),"Much of the success that has accompanied the move to block scheduling is due in a direct way to the willingness of teachers to make changes in their instructional methods . . . a structure for honest and open dialogue preceding implementation about the pros and cons."(p.8). We believe that the central office and the school administration must develop training and experimenting opportunities for instructional pacing and instructional strategies.

Once the course scope and sequence have been delineated, it is important to move to instructional alignment. The initial step for the classroom teacher when planning instruction is to develop a pacing guide or a listing of planned course topics to be taught in a semester. As previously stated, pacing guides detail the length of time needed to teach each content cluster and may also include resources, instructional methods, and individual student assignments. (See Example 1.) Many teachers question the purpose of developing a pacing guide, especially if they have never been involved in long-range planning for past courses. The value of a pacing guide is immeasurable as it aids teachers in making mental and instructional adjustment to a

EXAMPLE 1. 4X4 PACING GUIDE

Teacher:_____

Subject:_____

School:_____   Period:_____

Semester/Year:_____

Objectives, Skills, and Competencies	Instructional Strategy Activity and Procedures	Student Assessment
1.	1 - 10 Min. Review/Focus	1.
2.	10 - 30 Min. Instructional Objectives Presentations	2.
3.	30 - 60 Min. Interaction and Activities	3.
4.	60 - 80 Min. Reflections/ Comparisons/Debriefing	4.
5.	80 - 90 Closure/Summary	5.

blocked period and helps with planning for content relevance, student motivation and effective use of instructional time. The formation and evaluation of pacing guides will further help teachers succeed in the transitory phase and into the first year on the block by helping with the adjustment to the class time difference. Pacing guides can help teachers plan for the extended classes so that time is not wasted, but used completely. During the first year on a block, many teachers find that they are not completely successful in effectively utilizing every minute of a blocked period. The pacing guide can help teachers realize that more than one concept may be taught per day and will hopefully encourage effective planning so that the two or three concepts taught in one period are interrelated. The pacing guide will ultimately help teachers prevent losing any instructional time and aid them in the organization of their courses. (Specific details on how to design pacing guides and their benefits are presented in Chapter 9.)

STEP THREE: INSTRUCTIONAL STRATEGIES

Once the curriculum is aligned and appropriate pacing guides have been developed, it is time to learn several teaching strategies. Typically, in a "traditional schedule," teachers rely on lecture and note taking as primary instructional strategies, but this becomes monotonous and unmotivating to students if continued for extended periods of time (Day, Ivanov, & Binkley, 1996). Rettig and Canady (1996) assert that teachers in block schedules are able to plan lessons for extended periods of time and are motivated to use various instructional strategies other than lecture, such as learning centers, cooperative learning structures, and Socratic seminars. This may be true, but a prerequisite for the teacher is the ability to implement these types of strategies and methods of instruction. Many staffs have focused on content with little guidance in curriculum development and instructional methodology. Often it is assumed that teachers can make the transition to the block schedule, incorporating these techniques into their teaching without any training or modeling from other educators. Reid (1995) found that "most administrators thought that preparing teachers for the change was essential. Those who did not have inservice activities wished they had." Hence, a definite need for training addressing innovative teaching methods must be conducted.

The majority of the methods identified that are crucial for teaching extended periods focus on making learning more student-centered. Students are involved in activities that require their active input, not just passive listening and occasional note taking. There must be a "shift from the traditional lecture-and-discussion format of instruction to a more hands-on, project-oriented curriculum" (Day, Ivanov, & Binkley, 1996). The authors found that in schools using the 4x4 model, several teaching strategies are effective for the block schedules such as cooperative learning, the case method, Socratic seminars, synectics, concept attainment, inquiry, and simulation. According to Queen, Algozzine and Eaddy (1997), the development and use of many of these strategies in the 1980's led to the need for extended class time, becoming a catalyst for block scheduling and other scheduling alternatives. In this study, we recommend changing the class structure every 20–30 minutes and structure most lessons with a degree of great variability.

Block Scheduling which seems to be sweeping educational reforms nationwide is proven to benefit both the teacher and student. There has been a flourish of positive outcomes which is a direct result of block scheduling. From our experience with teachers and students we think the 4x4 block schedule will lead the way. The 4x4 block can give teachers a chance to arrange more creative and hands-on approach to learning which stimulates the students interest and in-class participation, so both sides benefit. Both the teacher and student have the opportunity to know each other personally, which eliminates the conflict that often accompanies a "lack" of communication. Block scheduling can address individual needs and teachers can be more creative in their instruction. As the class periods are extended, the teacher has time to thoroughly explain instructional time for the students, and the students are given the opportunity to learn more and ask questions that had been ignored in the past, due to the lack of time, flexibility, and a voice in their education which can create a focused group of learners.

Varied instructional strategies enable the student in a blocked class to learn on many different levels. In past surveys we have taken, students reported that one of the things they most liked about the block was the way their teachers taught. Students reported a drop in lecture and an increase in more hands-on activities. (See Graphs 1 and 2.) Before moving to the block, the chief concern students had about blocked classes was the fear of becoming bored. To maintain high levels of interest and address learning styles, teachers must plan detailed lessons which may include demonstrations, discussions, cooperative learning, the synectics model, case method, inquiry method, and other high-interest models.

After teachers learn to implement various strategies for teaching in the block, it is imperative to learn to assess the various methods. Therefore new means of assessing students must be addressed in staff development programs. Wyatt (1996) says teacher training should include such assessment methods as demonstrations, portfolios, and open-ended projects that "reflect students work and present the results of their learning in far more integrated, real-life applications." Likewise, the authors suggest similar ways of assessing students' progress when using varied teaching methods, all of which teachers should receive training for implementation. The assessment methods suggested are compiling portfolios, doing group and individual projects, completing surveys, and giving oral presentations. It is also essential for students to receive regular feedback regarding their progress in a class. Following staff development in various teaching methods should be training for assessing student progress as evidenced by participation in various activities.

The authors believe that before a faculty moves to any form of a block schedule, the teachers need to complete at least a week of workshops about appropriate pacing, course alignment, teaching strategies, and subject appropriate strategies. It is important that teachers receive training in not only pacing guide development and adaptation, but also in revising their own teaching strategies and learning new ones. The development of pacing guides helps teachers plan the time to be spent on each topic in a course, which is detrimental to the success of the conversion to block scheduling.

GRAPH 1. WHAT PERCENTAGE OF CLASS TIME DO YOUR TEACHERS SPEND IN INTERACTIVE INSTRUCTION?

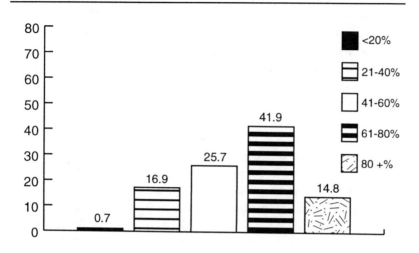

GRAPH 2. WHAT PERCENTAGE OF CLASS TIME DO YOUR TEACHERS SPEND MANAGING BEHAVIOR PROBLEMS?

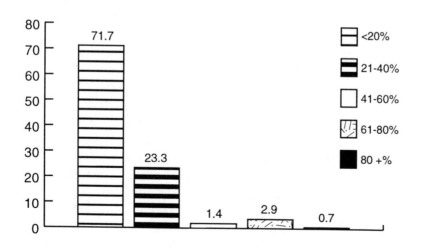

It is important when a change of this magnitude occurs within a school that a peer support community be built to provide the means by which all can learn and grow. The sharing of successes and failures with one another in "an ongoing informal basis is probably one of the most effective learning opportunities available for teachers (Wyatt, 1996). Meeting in larger groups also allows teachers to share effective lessons and brainstorm creative teaching approaches. Reid (1995) suggests that one of the ways to ease into the change of block scheduling is to provide common planning periods for departments in the first year. This allows teachers to share successful strategies and activities among their colleagues. Similarly, Hackmann (1995) suggests that faculty "form study groups to read and discuss literature" concerning educational change. He says that teachers in these groups can share journal articles and video tapes; attend state and national conferences; invite educators who have implemented block schedules to come and speak candidly about any obstacles they have overcome. Schools can meet with other schools implementing block scheduling on a regular basis, particularly by content groups, just to share ideas. A means of setting up a peer support group of some type is an essential element that should be set into place during staff development programs for schools converting to block scheduling.

One other type of staff development to learn additional instructional strategies is to establish a system to observe others teaching in the block schedule format. Fitzpatrick and Mowers (1997) state that "visiting a block school is more valuable than attending a presentation or reading articles." They contend that observers can see school climate, teaching techniques, and how teachers and students really feel about the schedule. Observing others allow teachers to see models of successful practice which will help teachers develop their courses and class structure effectively in response to a new schedule. DuFour (1997) asserts that peer observation should be common practice for all teachers. He says teachers should "receive training in classroom observation, instructional analysis, and conferencing skills to help them function as effective peer observers." This will not only improve their own methods, but give the observed teachers feedback to improve their strategies. In light of this, staff development programs should include a schedule for teachers to observe others inside their school and teachers in other schools that use the block schedule. Finally, development programs should also include training in observation skills.

When implementing block scheduling, it is important for schools to provide adequate staff development programs for teachers to adjust to the new time allotments. Wyatt (1996) says that staff development designed to influence what is planned for block classes will increase significantly the likelihood of better instruction. If the purpose of block scheduling is to make class time more effective learning time, then improved instruction and the ability to use longer time effectively are necessities. Specific procedures for lesson design and instructional strategies for use in the 4x4 block schedule are presented in chapter 10.

REFERENCES

Brett, M. (1996, February). Teaching extended class periods. *Social Education, 60*, 77–79.

Canady, R. L., & Reina, J. M. (1993). Parallel block scheduling: An alternative structure. *Principal, 72*, 26–29.

Day, M. M., Ivanov, C. P., & Binkley, S. (1996). Tackling block scheduling. *Educational Leadership, 53*, 24–27.

DuFour, R. P. (1997). The school as a learning organization: Recommendations for school improvement. *NASSP Bulletin, 81*, 81–87.

Fitzgerald, R. (1996, September). Brain-compatible teaching in a block schedule. *The School Administrator, 53*, 20–21,30.

Fitzpatrick, J. E., & Mowers, M. (1997). Success and the four block schedule: Stakeholders buy in! *NASSP Bulletin, 81*, 51–56.

Fullan, M. (1993). *Changing forces: Probing the depths of educational reform.* London: Falmer Press.

Hackmann, D. G. (1995). Ten guidelines for implementing block scheduling. *Educational Leadership, 53*, 24–27.

Hackmann, D.R. & Schmitt, D.M. (1997, April). Strategies for teaching in a block-of time schedule. *NASSP Bulletin*, 1–9.

Hoffman, E. (1995). A closer look at block scheduling. *Teaching Music, 2*, 42–43.

Huff, A. (1995). Flexible block scheduling: It works for us! *NASSP Bulletin, 79*, 19–22.

Jones, R. (1995, August). *Wake up! The Executive Educator, 17*, 14–18.

Queen, J. A., Algozzine, R. F., & Eaddy, M. A. (1997). The road we traveled: Scheduling in the 4 x 4 block. *NASSP Bulletin, 81*, 88–99.

Queen, J. A., & Gaskey, K. A. (1997). Steps for improving school climate in block scheduling. *Phi Delta Kappan, 79*, 158-161.

Reid, L. (1995). *Perceived effects of block scheduling on the teaching of English.* Fort Collins, CO: Colorado State University. (ED 382950).

Rettig, M. D. & Canady, R. L. (1996). All around the block: The benefits and challenges of a non-traditional school schedule. *The Administrator, 53*, 8–12.

Senge, P. (1990). *The fifth dimension: The art and practice of the learning organization.* New York: Doubleday Press.

Winans, D. (1996, April). Things go better with blocks. *NEA Today 14*, 13.

Wyatt, L.D. (1996). More time, more training. *The School Administrator, 53*, 16–18.

4

TRANSITIONS: THE THIRD STAGE IN IMPLEMENTING THE 4X4 BLOCK MODEL

STEP ONE: MAINTAINING FACULTY CONFIDENCE IN THE TRANSITION TO THE 4X4 BLOCK

As we previously stated, promises must be made by the committee and administration to the faculty that the change process will be deliberate and will progress cautiously. The faculty should not move hastily into a new schedule without proper training. Collecting research, visiting schools, and completing appropriate training will take one to two years. During these planning years, various opportunities for training should include mastering at least six major instructional strategies, realigning curriculum for instructional pacing, and establishing a schoolwide discipline program to ensure a safe school. A different option for transition would be to move at a slower pace and blocking one grade at a time. For example, one grade level could serve as a pilot to move to the block a year prior to the remainder of the school. This allows a school to remove many barriers to success prior to schoolwide implementation of the block. It is our belief that ninth grade serves best for this initial experiment in that transitions from middle school to high school are often in need of modification. Ninth grade students have the greatest difficulty in adjusting to any high school environment. Therefore, it would be reasonable to prepare these students for two major transitions: adjusting to high school and to a blocked format. If it is not logical for a school to block only one grade level, certain courses such as civics or English could be taught in double periods to simulate a block. Eventually, the tenth, eleventh and twelfth grades could follow with the implementation of the block model. Experimenting with the block for a year is an excellent way to test longer blocks of time and create experts within your own school. Teachers can observe the blocked classes of ninth grade or selected teachers to see the rate of progress. The remaining faculty should assist and move the program along to even greater success.

It is worth repeating, that the primary importance in change is establishing teacher support. This can be done by gaining teacher confidence and removing all insecurity about making a move to the new schedule design. Preparation and spending the required time for training will promote higher levels of motivation, comfort, and competence. Over the course of the transition, teacher confidence will also increase; however, teachers will have to make adaptations in curriculum, instruction, and pedagogy. It is our opinion that this adaptation is imperative for maximum success.

STEP TWO: MAINTAINING EFFECTIVE COMMUNICATION WITH TEACHERS

Often the biggest problem in making a successful transition to any block scheduling model has been the lack of communication between the administration and the faculty. Administrators must monitor classes on a daily basis and provide appropriate feedback and guidance to teachers. As teachers experiment with new instructional strategies, we recommend that for the first year there be some type of experimental opportunity for observations without any negative repercussions. Teachers should use the first year to master instructional strategies and to restructure their pacing guides. If teachers strive to improve teaching practices with this new model, they must not be penalized for errors. From years of successful training in block scheduling, we support and recommend observations that are experimentally free or non-threatening in order to promote better teaching as long-range goals. Obviously, if trying a new strategy that ends in disaster and results in a negative evaluation, the teacher may be hesitant to try alternative methods in the future. It is imperative to give teachers the first year for experimentation in a nonthreatening environment.

Communication between teachers is a plus when experienced teachers can help newer teachers work in teams as a committee and in harmony with the administration. The committee can be a vital tool in maintaining effective communication and monitoring success and serves to keep the administration aware of developing activities and concerns. The meetings between this committee and the administration should occur on a regular basis. Communication must be two-way when dealing with individual problems and schoolwide problems. Individual teaching problems and issues of personnel must be a function of the administration. Maintaining effective communication should include frequent classroom visits and encouragement by the administration. Following up with written statements, each faculty meeting should include a period of time allocated for talk on block scheduling success stories and problem issues. Remember, maintaining effective communication is accomplished by keeping an open two-way exchange. We have found this to be central to the success of block scheduling.

If there are several high schools in the county or system moving to the block, we recommend that a superintendents council be established. Two elected representatives from each school would serve on the council. Along with teachers and the superintendent, the council could also include building administration representatives and the associate superintendent of curriculum. The focus of the council would be on accessing the progress of the block, as it can become a forum for success stories and effective practice sharing. All of these things will help keep communication flowing. We recommend avoiding all large group confrontations and highlight administrative observations in the classroom on a consistent, daily basis.

STEP THREE: MONITORING FOR PROGRAM SUCCESS

When monitoring for success, administrators should search for improved instructional techniques, successful classroom experiences, the level to which scores are impacted, and the extent to which students are adjusting to the block model. It is important to keep students involved and to monitor their feelings about the block and their classes. (Student communication will be addressed in chapter 6.)

Following the first year, administrators should begin evaluating with a greater degree of teacher accountability, but the move to this type of observation and assessment should be gradual. The key to scheduling success is to monitor for the effective use of instructional strategies and practices that have been proven to work in extended periods. One final note: We strongly recommend that administrators monitor for teacher misuse of the last 30 minutes of class on a habitual basis. From our research, these final minutes of class time are habitually abused by at least 30 percent of school faculty in schools using block scheduling.

5

THE COMMUNITY: THE FOURTH STAGE IN IMPLEMENTING THE 4X4 BLOCK MODEL

STEP ONE: ESTABLISHING AND MAINTAINING COMMUNITY SUPPORT

After teacher acceptance of the block scheduling model, it is time to gain the support of the community and the student population. Our view at this point is that one should not necessarily precede the other. Quite honestly, both the community and parents are just as important as students with respect to input and involvement with the process. However, it is obviously most important and practical to have the teachers' support of the program prior to discussing the concept with students and parents.

The community and parents should be notified at the same time that students are notified of the block scheduling model. It would be most appropriate to send a letter home the same day students are notified, which defines and describes the concepts of the block. Some schools have an open forum where information is presented about block scheduling and concludes with a question-and-answer session. However, in a community-type setting, it is imperative to keep the session on the topic of the block model. Allowing a complaining or griping session of all the ills of education to emerge could have a negative impact on decisions. From our experience, we conclude that community and student support are important, but it is not mandatory that there be 100 percent support. This should be an educational decision with student and community support.

There are several effective ways to introduce concepts to parents. Make sure initial letters or newsletters are sent home in a timely fashion. We suggest that parents be notified at least a year in advance to introduce them to the concept of block scheduling. A second method of introduction should be during a parent/student night, which would provide an opportunity for questions. Distribute a set of predicted questions and the answers or a pamphlet of data on school success stories. Offer parents a look at the pros and cons of block scheduling. Also, keep sending updated information home on a weekly or monthly basis to inform parents of the steps taken in moving to block scheduling. Finally, develop a school-based or community-based committee that is made up of parents, students, and community leaders. Mature and well- respected student members could produce positive effects.

STEP TWO: PRESENTING BLOCK SCHEDULING TO PARENTS AND THE COMMUNITY

Unlike the faculty, parents are not quite as accessible to chat with casually about the possibilities of block scheduling. Parents will be presented with the new schedule after teachers have decided to move to the new program. The parents will be a large part of the transition, but they do not hold the deciding vote. When presenting block scheduling to parents and the community, we have found that it may take several repeat performances to various audiences to ensure education of the total community. A main presentation should be made during a schoolwide parent/teacher meeting and followed by smaller presentations to the band boosters, the athletic boosters, athletic games, and a course fair.

Approaching parents with a new idea for their child's high school schedule can be quite precarious if not handled carefully. Positive attitudes must prevail in order to reassure parents that the move has been carefully planned, that teachers are ready, and that students will benefit.

The parent/student night presentations could include:

♦ panel discussion of teachers, parents, and students currently using a block schedule.

♦ a general introduction of the concept of the specific block scheduling model, what it will mean to the individual child, and what it means for the future.

♦ the distribution of a graphic representation of a 4x4 schedule.

♦ an announcement of the curriculum fair or festival where each department displays new courses, required courses, and possibilities for future courses.

Some schools have arranged a spaghetti dinner fund raiser and meeting to introduce the new schedule or preceded the meeting with student performances. Often student delegations that have made visits to block schools perform skits for the introductory night.

STEP THREE: GAINING PARENT AND COMMUNITY SUPPORT

When establishing a plan to gain parent support and community acceptance of a move to a block schedule, some guidelines apply. The quickest way to lose support is to keep new scheduling plans a secret. There should be no reason to keep information away from the community. We have seen major problems of mistrust develop. For example, we are aware of the failure of one program where a school system decided to make a major curricular change without informing parents and the community. A concerned group of parents discovered the school system's plans for the change and were alarmed that they had not been informed. The negative feelings were perpetuated by press reports which seemed to magnify the situation and ultimately led to the waste of thousands of dollars and the removal of the new program. Keeping parents informed is the number one rule. It is not imperative to ask the permission of parents, but it is important to inform them of the transition to a block schedule. Educators are the professionals who serve students and their parents, so the idea is to ask for parent input or support only.

To ensure success, identify the active parents or community supporters who are proactive and open to new ideas. Usually the band/music boosters, the athletics boosters, the academic boosters, and the parent/teacher organization are supported by informed and caring parents. Use these key people and other well-respected parents in the community to serve on a parent committee. The committee should consist of parents from all areas in the community and be diverse. Again, it is important to note that this committee is only advisory and does not have the final vote on the adoption of the block model.

Community acceptance could also be gained by getting government officials behind the new schedule. The support of the local mayor, the city council, and the school board, along with church leaders can bring quick acceptance and success for the program. Once the coveted support is gained, however, maintaining that support can be accomplished by keeping parents informed and involved in the process of change.

Every week a short newsletter should go home with students, that explains the stages of transition to a block schedule. Include scheduling strengths, training schedules, reports of visits to other schools, a basic overview of the improvement process, and ways parents can help. Often parents can support programs financially as well as offer physical help. Attaining parental assistance with the athletic program, the school building, or with various school trips should be accomplished early as volunteers may find it difficult to get out of obligations at the last minute. Careful planning to involve parents may even move beyond the bounds of the school committee for reform. A separate parental involvement committee will increase the likelihood of substantial parental volunteerism.

The parent and community awareness of block scheduling may also be presented outside of the school in community cen-

ters, houses of worship or the YMCA. This relocation of introductory meetings may allow community members to speak to
the principal on a one-on-one basis. Community support will
be generated by elective courses designed with a community
service element. There is an excellent opportunity to institute a
volunteer program in the block schedule, especially in the junior or senior year, that involves one or two periods of community service activity. Parents will see that true community service
teaches not only responsibility, but learning skills which may
result in future employment.

Another area of importance in maintaining parent support
is that of teacher training. Highlight teacher training and resultant possibilities for the community and students in the weekly
newsletters and community newspapers. Allay any fears parents may have of students spending hours and hours in classes
of lecture. The greatest misconception parents and students have
about the block is student boredom. Reassure parents that
teacher training for the lengthened classes includes the use of
various instructional strategies and class pacing for effective
instruction. Teachers will learn how to use the 90 minutes (or
longer) to benefit each student and his or her learning needs.

STEP FOUR: KEEPING THE MEDIA INFORMED

To present the schedule to the media, a simple fact sheet can
be developed for reporters or to serve as a guide for administrators and teachers in interviews. Several short fact sheets could
be developed to keep the media up-to-date on the transition
steps to the block. A sample fact sheet may appear as follows:

1. **Timeline:** In February, American High School plans
on taking a delegation of teachers, students, and parents to several high schools currently utilizing the 4x4
block scheduling model. This delegation will report its
findings during a parent/student/teacher meeting later
that month. In March, the teachers and students are
going to participate in a curriculum fair which will be
open to the public. Visit the fair for food, dramatic presentations, music, and course information for next year.

The fair will take place two weeks prior to the guidance and registration period for the next school year. In May and June, the faculty of American High School will participate in workshops to develop new pacing guides and to learn exciting instructional strategies.

2. Definition of Block Scheduling: The 4x4 block scheduling model, which American High School is moving to next school year, enables students to enroll in eight classes per year instead of six. Students take four courses first semester and four courses second semester. The classes are blocked, lasting for a 90-minute block of time, enabling students to have more in-depth, hands-on learning. Teachers have time to address the learning needs of various learners and will not just lecture for the entire period! Usually, it is helpful to present a graphic example of the school day to see the structure of the coming school year.

Sample 4x4 Schedule for a Ninth Grade Student

First Semester	Second Semester
First Period English I	First Period Physical Science
Second Period Algebra I	Second Period Civics/Geography
Lunch	Lunch
Third Period Chorus	Third Period Spanish I
Fourth Period Keyboarding I	Fourth Period Geometry

Sample 4x4 Schedule for an Eleventh Grade Student

First Semester	Second Semester
First Period English III	First Period Chemistry
Second Period Algebra III	Second Period Speech
Lunch	Lunch
Third Period Auto Mechanics	Third Period American History
Fourth Period Spanish III	Fourth Period Auto Mechanics

3. Training Announcement: American High School teachers and the administration are participating in a block scheduling training workshop taught by J. Allen Queen and Kim Gaskey Isenhour, authors of *Steps for Improving School Climate in Block Scheduling* (*Phi Delta Kappan*, October, 1997). The purpose of the workshop will be to learn how to best utilize the 4x4 block scheduling model for American High School students. The teachers are very excited for the opportunity to plan courses in the new schedule and to use many of the innovative instructional strategies taught in the workshop.

Training will include specific pacing workshops for the new time frame which will ensure that the curriculum will be taught and that no required skills will be omitted. Training will also include effective teaching strategies for the block schedule, which means students will be challenged and not bored by a 90-minute lecture class. American High School teachers are so excited about the new schedule and the possibilities for student success. Included are photos of our teachers actively involved in training. (Teachers may want to keep these photos for the yearbook and the school newspaper.)

4. Introducing the 4x4 in Parent/Student Meetings: Next Tuesday night at 7:00 PM, American High School will be hosting a parent/teacher/student meeting on the possibilities for a new schedule. A team of teachers, students, and administrators will present their findings on the 4x4 block scheduling model already in use by many schools across the country. The meeting will be held in the gymnasium.

5. Curriculum Fair or Other Introductory Presentation: American High School will hold a curriculum fair this Friday night from 6:00 PM until 9:00 PM. Performing will be members of the drama club, the symphonic band, the jazz band, and the senior chorus. Members of the art club will be drawing caricatures and the vocational department will team up with the foreign language department to provide cuisine from around the world. Please attend to learn more about the course changes for next year, possible mentorships/apprenticeships/internships, and new elective courses.

6. Registration: Registration for the new school year will be held over the next two weeks. Guidance counselors will travel to American Middle School to register incoming freshmen, and our students will have individual appointments with their assigned counselors. Students should be sure to come prepared with a plan of courses they would like to take during their high school years.

7. The First Days: The reactions of teachers and students to the new schedule accompanied by photos of students engaged in learning are a hot topic for the opening of school. All of the preparations have been made and the benefits of the transition process will become evident as the first year progresses.

The maintenance of parental acceptance requires early involvement of a community advisory committee. It is key to the transitional process to keep parents abreast of the exciting changes, to seek help from parents, to observe successful block programs, and to elicit parental support in the preparation of the physical structure of the school.

One phenomenon educators need to be aware of is the honeymoon period involved in starting new programs. Often when new programs are started, educators are active in their efforts to gain the support of parental involvement, input, financial support, and volunteerism. After the honeymoon period is over, parents are often left out of the loop of information and involvement. This can be avoided if the committee formed elects a liaison team to meet with the principal or with the chair of the school-based teacher committee. Another way to avoid the isolation following the initial implementation period is by the effective use of newspapers and newsletters that relate more than just the basics of the program. Real success stories from each subject area could be written by teachers from various disciplines on a weekly basis. Also, the parent group can provide a newsletter from their perspective on a monthly basis.

STEP FIVE: MAINTAINING EFFECTIVE COMMUNICATION WITH PARENTS

Develop a brochure or introduction flier for the school which includes the school slogan, an open invitation to the school, possible mentorships, apprenticeships, and business partnerships, and possibilities for post-secondary study. Slogan adoption and the marketing of T-shirts or bumper stickers can help make the school visible to parents and students. Football games, held early in the year, are well attended by parents and provide an excellent opportunity to inform parents of the block scheduling model. Teachers can operate a question-and-answer booth at the football games to offer information about courses, block scheduling, the reason the change was made, and the way to become involved. In this booth, include sign-ups for booster organizations, parent/teacher organizations, tutors, and volunteers.

To gain parental support for the block, we have recommended a partnership with local newspapers and the distribution of a weekly or bi-weekly parent newsletter. This print medium of communication with parents is vital in the process of informing parents of the new program.

A parent/community survey issued at the end of every year will keep the communication flow going in both ways. With respect to parent/community surveys it is important to keep leaders and groups actively involved who will keep the principal's ear full of pertinent information. Usually, there will be a small group of highly active parents and teachers who will be involved in every step of the reformation. Therefore, it is important to send home parent surveys during various periods of time. The first should be right after the end of the first semester of the block. This allows parents to get a sense of how the block feels and allow them to express their ideas or ventilate any feelings or concerns they may have early in the year. This release prevents small problems from becoming large impediments to the success of the school. A second survey should be sent out at the end of the spring semester during the first year and from then on, one survey at the end of the year will do. It is most likely that schools will only get back 25–30 percent of the surveys distributed. One way to maximize the community return rate is to send the surveys home in large folders /envelopes with cardboard to keep the bubble sheets or other response forms from being damaged. These could be given out during homeroom or first period and returned the next day. If parents or anyone surveyed has a week or two to return, the return rate will not be as high as when the survey is due back the following day.

Communication with parents through letters is another tool in keeping parents informed about the transition process. Open forums and monthly meetings will be a valuable tool for principals to use as well.

Teacher attitude will make or break schedules. Teachers living in the community who make visits to the local dry cleaners or the grocery store may be able to clear up strange rumors about the new schedule and create or spread a positive attitude about moving to the schedule. If the teachers are motivated to share the good news about the new schedule, the community will benefit from this shared knowledge.

In gaining the acceptance of parents and students, the listing of valuable results to the individual students helps to bring the transition process into every home. The students and parents are able to clearly state what the schedule will do for them. When thinking about this in terms of the community, we should ask: what can the block model do for local companies? Block scheduling gives schools the ability to form more realistic and meaningful relationships with local businesses. The physical education teacher may offer a weekly aerobics class for teachers and workers from the local textile mill in exchange for periodic tours by students. Business sponsorships by companies can be a mutually beneficial prospect. Businesses have their name printed on school documents, on school signs, and in the newspaper announcing the connection with the local school. Positive public relations and the use of support as an advertising tool will be the rewards for businesses. For the schools, monetary aid, technical assistance, and apprenticeship/ mentorship programs are the gains.

In addition to surveys, communication with parents through letters is another tool in keeping parents informed about the transition process. Various types of letters from different school leaders to parents may be necessary. The following sample letters can be modified to fit the needs of any school.

Sample A. Letter of introduction from principal and faculty of the school.

Dear Parents:

For the past several years, American High School has been actively restructuring its program of studies to better meet the needs of all students. We believe that our efforts are helping students to prepare themselves for a rapidly changing and more sophisticated work place.

The next phase in our restructuring plan will be implemented during the upcoming school year when our teachers will be delivering our curriculum in four 90-minute classes each day. In this format, students will receive one unit of credit for each class per semester, with a possible total of eight units per year. Our teachers have been involved in scheduling research and have visited numerous schools currently utilizing the 4x4 block scheduling model. They are extremely excited about the possibilities the schedule will provide for students and have reported evidence of proven success from many schools on the 4x4.

During the next few weeks, we intend to inform our students and parents about our plan to move to the 4x4 block schedule. To facilitate a smooth transition and to answer any questions you may have, a meeting is scheduled for Monday, March 10, at 6:30 PM in the gymnasium. Members of the staff and of the American High Student Council will address any questions or concerns you may have. Please plan to attend this meeting and discover our plans for future success.

Sincerely,

John Q. Principal, Jr.
Principal, American High School

Included with this initial letter is a list of the most often asked questions and answers about block scheduling:

1. Why is American High School considering a move from the traditional schedule?

We are making plans to change to a 4x4 block schedule to better meet the needs of our students who find themselves in a more demanding curriculum and are looking toward a more sophisticated workplace. Research indicates that the current schedule of 55-minute classes is a major obstacle to the learning process. The current schedule fosters lecture-style classes with an emphasis on covering the material rather than mastering it. In addition, an enormous waste of time and energy is expended by students moving all over the building five or six times a day, not to mention the discipline problems inherent in class changes.

Further, we can reduce class size, decrease daily loads for students and teachers, increase the number of courses available and the number taken, if we change to a four-period day. Under a traditional schedule, teachers teach five classes per year. Under the 4x4 model, teachers teach six classes a year, thereby increasing the number of classes offered by 20 percent. The total number of students in a day with whom a teacher has contact could decrease as much as 30 percent, and the number of students taught in a full year could increase by 33 percent.

2. Why choose the 4x4 plan and not some other block scheduling model?

Several scheduling models are used in schools across the nation. The A/B schedule, the Copernican Plan or modified block, and the 4x4 were all researched. Advantages of the 4x4 schedule include: expanded course selections, reduced course load for students (four classes a day instead of six), opportunities for immediate remediation, less time wasted on "administrative matters" and class changes, more opportunities for hands-on activities, labs, and small-group activities, and longer class time with the same teacher.

3. How will this schedule effectively meet the needs of students who are at-risk academically?

During a 90-minute period, teachers will be able to vary teaching methods to address diverse learning styles. Teachers could include cooperative learning, synectics, case method, seminar teaching, technology, discovery learning, centers, guest speakers, interdisciplinary teaching, class period field trips, as well as lecture in their course. Science labs and other project-oriented activities could be completed in one period, thereby maintaining interest, instead of dragging them out over several days.

Students will focus on four courses rather than six. Every attempt will be made to balance schedules to include at least two academic classes and two electives per semester. All students should be able to receive individual attention in the longer period and get to know their teachers better.

4. How will this schedule benefit students who are high achievers?

Traditionally, students have been restricted to certain courses because of college entrance requirements. Consequently, they have often been unable to take advantage of vocational, performing arts, or other interest area courses. Too often, because of our school size and limited number of elective courses, students have had to choose between two courses that were important to them. With the addition of two courses each year, students can upgrade their academics and take advantage of other elective opportunities. In a four year career, students can almost be guaranteed of getting every course they desire.

5. Will more elective courses be offered?

Yes. American High will be able to offer several new courses such as a SAT/PSAT preparation course, journalism, creative writing, drama, foreign language courses beyond the second level, aerobics, and astronomy. These courses, along with many other vocational courses, will be added on a yearly basis.

6. How can the same amount of material be taught in one semester when it takes an entire year now?

The course will last for one semester, but the actual time spent in class will be 90 minutes per day instead of only 55 minutes. Teachers currently involved in block scheduling have found that they are able to cover more information in a longer class period than they would in two regular class periods. This phenomenon is due to fewer interruptions and fewer "starting and stopping" activities.

SAMPLE B: Letter announcing advisement period and class fair from guidance office.

Dear Parents and Students:

American High School will begin its yearly registration process beginning on March 31. The implementation of a new schedule, the 4x4 block scheduling model, requires that careful attention be given to each student's schedule. A balance of core academic courses and electives must be achieved between the two semesters. Long-term planning is also helpful to ensure that students are able to take the courses that they wish to take before graduation. Sequencing courses is very important. We do not want a student to take Spanish I during the first semester of his or her freshman year and then not take Spanish II until the second semester of his or her junior year.

A course festival/fair is planned for March 26 in the main concourse. All departments will display course materials, possible new electives, mentorship opportunities, intern jobs, and post-secondary partnerships. You are invited to attend the festival as it will help in planning your schedule for the next school year and subsequent years. Student work will be displayed and several drama, band, chorus, and vocational students will perform skills during the evening. The foreign language department and students from Mrs. Cook's parenting class will provide delicious appetizers.

Please make plans to join us at the curriculum fair at 7:00 PM in the main concourse on March 26. We are excited about next year and the great opportunities students will enjoy.

Sincerely,

Donna Q. Counselor
American High School Guidance Counselor

SAMPLE C: Letter from the principal to parents and students prior to the first year.

Dear Parents and Students:

After months of preparation, American High School is ready to start the new year on a 4x4 block schedule. Many of you participated in making our transition a smooth one, and the faculty and I would like to express our thanks for all your input. Teachers and students from schools using a block warned us that the first semester may be tiring at the start, but it will also be exciting for all involved. Your teachers have been involved in numerous training programs and will start the new year with engaging learning strategies.

Absences in the new schedule are quite harmful because of the large amount of work a student must make up. Be sure you start the new year with this in mind and ready to take advantage of all the great opportunities provided by the new schedule. To prevent students from falling behind, progress reports will be issued between report card periods and opportunities for tutoring posted throughout the year.

The faculty and I want to know what you think and we want to let the community know about your successes. Be sure to read the student newspaper and the monthly parent newsletter for updates on our progress throughout the year. We would love to have student and parent contributions to these documents!

Best wishes for a great year full of academic success. Let's make this first year on a block schedule something to remember! GO EAGLES!!

Sincerely,

John Q. Principal
Principal, American High School

SAMPLE D: Letter to parents and students prior to the second semester from the teacher site-based management team.

Dear Parents and Students:

Congratulations on a successful first semester! Grades from the first semester have been calculated and there has been a marked increase in scores. Our discipline referrals to the office have decreased and the school janitors are pleased with the cleanliness of the school grounds as compared with previous years.

Now that the excitement of a new schedule is waning, lets not allow the second semester scores to fall. Please continue your hard work and dedication to learning. Many students found that absences in the new schedule hurt their performance on tests and in daily participation. Don't let this happen to you this semester!

The first day of class for the second semester will be January 5. Our parent-teacher meeting for parents to get acquainted with the new second semester teachers will be held on January 18. Progress reports will be given out that night and the chorus will perform their award winning competition music presentation. Hope to see you there!

Keep up the good work this semester. We are proud of your success.

Sincerely,

Mr. Dave R. Teacher
Chairperson, Building Committee

Other letters to parents and students could include a description of survey results and letters sent prior to the opening of each subsequent school year. Depending on the content of the letter, parents will most likely receive the letter by mail or from their student.

6

THE STUDENTS:
THE FIFTH STAGE IN
IMPLEMENTING THE
4X4 BLOCK MODEL

STEP ONE: PRESENTING THE 4X4 BLOCK
SCHEDULE TO STUDENTS

Students need to be notified at the same time as parents about the adoption of the 4x4 block. This notification usually occurs a year or two prior to the program getting started. The students should assemble in the gymnasium or auditorium for a positive form of entertainment. During some kind of formal presentation, let students know there will be schedule changes to enable them a greater opportunity to choose interesting courses. Present the block model in a positive fashion. Mention block and its meaning, and talk to the students about individual benefits so that the new program is presented positively and early. In the three-year longitudinal study we conducted, students, teachers and administrators rated the success of the block. (See Graph 1.) Success stories like these will add a positive element to your initial presentation.

GRAPH 1. WOULD YOU RATE THE SUCCESS OF THE 4X4 AS
GOOD, FAIR OR POOR?

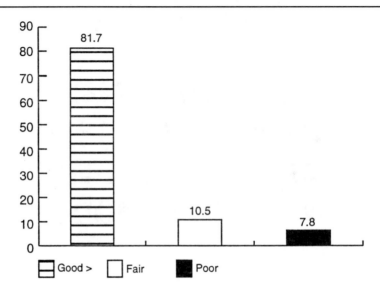

The presentation of the new model should take place at least
a year before the initiation of the new schedule. Prior to the holidays, students can be brought by classes for details on the design of the new day, the individual relevance it has for students,
and the increased graduation requirements. When making the
presentations to students it is effective to have student presenters. The student presenters should have made visits to schools
using the same type of block scheduling model. Introduction of
the new program by students can create a sense of ownership
and excitement about making a transition. Students usually highlight the opportunity to take various electives, the chance for
repeating courses in a single year, and taking a course for only
one semester. The students may elect student officers for a block
scheduling committee. This committee usually meets with the
administration to hear updated news, to discuss student concerns, and to reassure students of the benefits of the 90–120
minute class. The student committee, just as the parent committee, does not vote the block into acceptance, but it does have
input, asks questions, and shares concerns. Students are fair and

will examine the block in great detail. We found this to be a constant in all the block scheduling schools.

Once the group of selected students has learned all about the new model, gaining acceptance through meetings with various groups on campus is the next step. Question-and-answer sessions with student clubs is an excellent venue for sharing knowledge. Student input in the early stages of the transition process and student visits to schools on a block schedule where students talk to other students about the model are the best first steps for involving students. New dimensions or any change can often be better accepted by students if teachers do not present them as a positive negative thing. Block scheduling goes beyond the confines of a mere administrative tool or scheduling procedure. It has actually become a philosophical model.

STEP TWO: GAINING AND MAINTAINING STUDENT ACCEPTANCE

When trying to educate students and persuade them to see the benefits in block scheduling, success all comes down to the presentation. Focus on making the transition and the new schedule fresh, futuristic, exciting, and personally beneficial. A second step to the total school presentation of the model will be the use of student advocates. Student advocates could write articles in the student newspaper to introduce specific information about electives, to offer testimonials from students already on the block, and to describe a day in the life of a student. The student newspaper puts the scheduling terminology into a student voice.

Students readily accept the block model when they see what it will mean for them individually. Stressing the reality of the block to students works as students want the bottom line on how the schedule will affect them personally. Students like the ability to choose interesting classes and the reduction of tracking into one group of classes, as students now have more possibilities for personal choice with the eight periods per year. For example, students find that the 4x4 is similar to a college schedule in that classes last for only one semester. Teachers and students are energized about the program because the lengthened time allows for more project work, more hands-on activities, and more attention to individual interests. Another area of interest for students has been the school curriculum fair and possible participation in the fair.

STEP THREE: INCLUDING STUDENTS IN THE PROCESS OF TRANSITION

Visitation to participating schools creates student advocates or messengers with true knowledge of the program. Several student delegations may visit student government meetings in similarly blocked schools and report their findings to various clubs or during the parent/teacher/student meetings. Students selected to make site visits should be from every grade level and represent all social groups in the school. We recommend limiting seniors on the visits because they will graduate and will not experience the schedule. Representatives should be selected from the band, the vocational and art departments, one each from the ninth, tenth and eleventh grades, various clubs and sports teams. The student delegation should be representative of the diversity in the school and every social group on a campus. Every attempt should be made to select students who are open-minded and respond well in a democratic-oriented, school environment. Students who dislike school will be of limited assistance. Including students can be achieved through student delegations, but it is also highly effective to have students help in the general communication process with parents, the community and other students and in the evaluation of the new schedule.

STEP FOUR: MAINTAINING EFFECTIVE COMMUNICATION WITH STUDENTS

Students get a sense of involvement from the early stages of planning on large and small levels. Student representatives, two from each grade level can meet with the administration at predetermined times to periodically keep up-to-date on the transition. These meetings between students and principals give just as much insightful information as meetings between power executives from industry and their employees on the factory floor. The quality of the new schedule will be vastly improved through the relationship with students. Student representatives serve as an ear for principals to gain information, and, we have discovered, they function to disseminate information to other students. In a system where there are several schools on block, students serve on a superintendent's council. This council meets to accumulate information and gain support for the new model while establishing links between schools in the same system.

Another advisory situation is the creation of a summit meeting of selected students and teachers from each grade level from across an entire school system that meet to solicit ideas of future interest and share success stories. After any summit or superintendent's council meeting, the local newspaper should print student pictures and highlight student involvement in these activities. Communication is thus maintained between students, educators, parents, and the community. The individual school newspaper is the best place to communicate student opinion and perception of scheduling changes. To further hear the voice of all students, a survey should be administered to students after the first semester on a block schedule and after the first year. The survey results could reveal much needed reform in some areas, the feeling of great success, or a combination of both.

7

TEACHER INSERVICE: THE SIXTH STAGE IN IMPLEMENTING THE 4X4 BLOCK MODEL

STEP ONE: USING EXPERIENCED TRAINERS

During the early stages of development, there should be questions and discussion about who will conduct the actual training sessions. In most situations, school systems either bring in outside experts or they hire a team of teachers from another school that is using the block to train teachers. There are several advantages in hiring professional trainers.

Professional trainers are well researched and have skills and experience in presenting this information. They are viewed and received by teachers as experts. Experts have usually clarified or identified areas in the presentation of block information that may cause concern or problems that can occur in the block. Basically, they have the bugs worked out. This will save time but is well worth the expense. We have found that systems or schools who use their own trainers will have to complete hours of research and possibly travel extensively to gain sufficient knowledge to train teachers.

STEP TWO: CHECKING FOR CREDIBILITY

Scholars with experience receive a high degree of credibility. If the researcher has been published or has helped several school systems move to a block, and has extensive training, credibility is established. Usually the attendance and participation is higher when an outside professional is brought in to train the staff. People who have worked in a block for a couple of years will also have more credibility with teachers. However, we have found that there is a problem with using teachers from other schools. These teachers only highlight one or two concepts with a single successful strategy. They may have a good method for teaching a certain procedure or skill which may be effective for a single content area. The trainer may be quite competent in the methodologies, but the teachers in the session usually only receive a few ideas for class and do not expand those ideas from training into the classroom. We have found that these receiving teachers do not get involved in curriculum alignment or pacing activities to an appropriate level. Usually reliable trainers who have worked with schools will take the process approach of curriculum alignment, pacing guides, and instructional alignment through all processes. Instructional strategies may be taught at one time to a large group. There may be selected strategies that work better or in different ways for certain content areas. For example, inquiry method can work in numerous classes and does not need to be limited to the science class.

STEP THREE: SELECTING APPROPRIATE TRAINERS

If the school system decides to use selective teachers, it is recommended that those teachers spend a great deal of time observing master teachers who have taught in a similar block model for several years. Use videotaped lessons in the training. Strategies are difficult to transfer because much is lost from indirect observations. If there are excellent teachers who are willing to serve as lead trainers, they may be well received. These teachers have not actually worked in a block. Therefore, they may be valued in the school for their teaching ability, but not trusted in the transition to the block. There will always be some doubt as to whether this new schedule will work. Bringing in experts or people who have been successful in the block for years will negate the degree of doubt that may exist. We recommend that experts well known in the field or excellent teachers from local schools on a block be used in all major training sessions. Make sure that those teachers have a leader to open the sessions and give a building or background session to start the training. We do not recommend the use of teachers from in-house. It does not give credibility needed for success.

STEP FOUR: PREPARING TRAINING MATERIALS

When developing training sessions, trainers will need such basics as overhead projectors, a screen, newsprint, pens, chalkboards, and flipcharts to use for instruction. Having these items ready prior to the workshop is extremely important. It is essential to find out what each trainer will need for his or her presentations. You may have someone working with certain content areas that will require materials very different from other presenters. Money should be set aside for copy materials, the development of notebooks, pacing guides, and lesson plan designs. Many school systems rent copy machines to make the copies necessary for training. We believe this is acceptable. However, teachers should develop their own pacing guides. Teachers can use samples from trainers and specific handouts for activities can be productive. Copies of contracts, rubrics, classroom management guides, safe school plans, etc., are excellent to share. Teachers will need to bring materials for taking notes, all textbooks, and other supplementary materials to use in the training sessions. We have found that pacing guide sections or lesson plans from previous years are extremely helpful.

Other needs of teachers and trainers must also be addressed. Teachers should have coffee, refreshments, light breakfast, snack, and lunch. In past training sessions, some school systems have provided lunch, allowed teachers to leave campus to purchase their own lunch, or required a deposit for a special luncheon on campus. Obviously, administrators can save money if teachers have lunch on their own. This will save money over a long training session. The physical environment must also be pleasing and comfortable for the trainers and the teachers. School systems may hold the training in a central facility, a high school library, in individual classes, in rented spaces, or in a retreat location. Often businesses or civic organizations will provide facilities at no cost.

STEP FIVE: SCHEDULING INSERVICE ACTIVITIES

For the initial training, we suggest that it be completed at least a year in advance of the move to the block. Ample time is needed for the training. Practically every system or school we have worked with underestimated the needed training. The training that begins the year should include curriculum alignment followed by pacing guide development. Usually this can be accomplished in the summer prior to the year of preparation. For example, a June training session on curriculum alignment and pacing can be followed by a year of instructional strategies and assessment training. It takes the most time to focus on the beginning stage. Usually what happens here is the faculty or central office training organizers need to decide if the initial training should be done in a location away from the school campus. Some schools may decide to go on a retreat to kick off the transition to a block. The training can then be an intense two or three days of workshops away from the telephones and other distractions of campus life. This focusing of effort is advantageous and is important, but teachers should not work to a high level of fatigue and stress. Working long days and pushing to complete guides in these days will not produce the quality needed. Make sure there is ample time for social activities. The activities should be diverse to provide teachers a choice: hiking, fishing, horseback riding, shopping, movies, etc. The socialization process is extremely important for success. Teachers must develop a strong sense of trust from working with one another. This will help boost morale and build effective teams. The time and effort is concentrated, and there is not a constant pull for a teacher's time. It is important to look into the cost of a retreat. It can be quite expensive when paying for the rent of the meeting location, the trainers' expenses, teachers' lodging, food and entertainment.

We have discovered that training can be effective on or off campus. Schools may use the local community center, church, local businesses, or meeting place for a mini-retreat. Perimeters must be set to focus on the training. Costs of travel expenses and overnight stays will not have to be paid if a local retreat location is used. This savings may allow a school system to bring in more trainers or better qualified trainers. This is only with the initial training. There should be some component of training all year long, with a weekly update in the faculty meeting or other meeting time.

Time during the year must be set aside to plan for the move. Early release days, teacher work days, and after-school departmental meetings can be designated during the year for activities or formal training sessions. Teachers who have similar course content enjoy planning together. It allows them to utilize expertise in a particular area and expand upon their strategies and lesson plans. Teachers can share ideas and share plans if they teach similar subjects. Many teachers will use similar techniques in a discipline and can directly aid first-year teachers in their department. It is important to have departmental meetings in every stage of the training, especially in curriculum alignment. Pacing guides can seem overwhelming to start, so planning as a department may be effective in the initial development of a guide. Every teacher should formulate his or her own guide, as all teachers have different delivery styles. One word of caution: do not permit teachers to merely go back to their classroom and work. Many times, even with the best intentions, teachers will work on pressing issues of the day and never get around to planning for the block.

The instructional strategies and techniques will be taught near the end of the school year and into the summer prior to the move to the block. The second summer may include time for a second retreat or special trainers. From the beginning, a master plan for training must be developed. The three stages should include preplanning, training and monitoring. In all three stages, there must be all elements of curriculum alignment, instructional pacing, instructional strategies and evaluations.

STEP SIX: SPECIAL NEEDS OF FIRST-YEAR TEACHERS

First-year teachers' training is extremely important. Many times it is valuable to perform this training in the school setting to allow for a degree of familiarity. From our experience, staff development personnel make no assumptions about students being well versed in block scheduling from educational classes. Although block scheduling is discussed, it is usually in the form of issues and not in the form of preparing future teachers to work in the block. Colleges and universities have not made adjustments to training future teachers for a block. Education of future teachers for the block in many universities may be analytical and evaluative rather than methodological. Courses in curriculum design and theory where students are involved in learning design may not be taught until graduate school. Many times first-year teachers will not have the background needed for curriculum alignment or for developing a functioning pacing guide. A mentor should be assigned to them to assist them in a partnership rather than an evaluative role. It is important that first-year teachers not be isolated from training because it would isolate them from the faculty.

8

PITFALLS AND PROMISES: THE SEVENTH STAGE IN IMPLEMENTING THE 4X4 BLOCK MODEL

STEP ONE: BEWARE OF THE SECOND SEMESTER PHENOMENON

Some of the problems that teachers often face at the end of the first semester involve feelings of doubt and concerns of completing a total year, and the experience of general fatigue. Some teachers feel more motivated in the first semester because of the "new" feeling of the schedule and the inherent challenge provided. After the first semester, teachers and students have completed in one semester what had been taught over the course of an entire year. This may cause teachers to feel a bit fatigued at the start of the second semester. For other teachers, the fatigue doesn't set in until late in the second semester.

STEP TWO: PREPARE TO GIVE EXAMS BEFORE CHRISTMAS BREAK

For schools with the 4x4 block, we recommend that exams be given before the Christmas break. This will ensure that the

Christmas holidays will be a true rest period. The new year will bring the excitement of a new semester, not the return to the end of the first semester. Teachers often feel like they have to start all over again with students that take exams after the holiday break. Fatigue is more likely for teachers and students if a review period and exams are then immediately followed by the first day of the second semester, without a break. In some cases, there may be a day or two for teachers to average grades, but other schools start the next semester the day after taking exams. This day-after start only causes confusion, tension, and lack of focus for all involved. The authors therefore strongly recommend that the first semester be completed before the Christmas break. This means that the school calendar will change: school will start earlier in August and end earlier in the spring.

Usually by the end of the first year, fatigue resulting from the change from one semester to another subsides. Teachers learn how to pace themselves and internalize the time changes. The second year will bring great success. Beginning teachers do not have this semester change fatigue. We believe this may be due to the fact or relationship of the similarities of college semester courses with the block semester courses.

STEP THREE: ADJUST THE SCHOOL CALENDAR

After the first year, it is valuable for teachers to assess the year. Teachers can also assess during the winter holidays to look for ways to improve their teaching skills. During the second year research has indicated a great deal of success. The teachers adapt their energy to an appropriate level for each semester. Many systems have taken our advice and have adjusted the school calendar to accommodate testing before the holidays. This adjustment requires that the first semester begin two to three weeks earlier than in years before the block. Systems can expect some strong opposition from faculty and staff of elementary and middle schools. We have found the problem to be not with the block, but with making the change too rapidly and without advanced notification to these staff members. Parents at all levels may be concerned initially since the early school starting date may interfere with summer or Labor Day vacations. We have found the solution to be quite simple. Involve parents and representative teachers from all school divisions to design two or three different recommendations of the new calendar for the new school year. Plan for the transition of time for the early start at least two years in advance. This may mean starting the first year on the old schedule, but having the support for the change the next year is an equitable exchange.

STEP FOUR: CAUTION—MEASURE SUCCESS AND ENERGY LEVELS

It has been our experience that the success of the program will equal the energy level that is put into the design, implementation and maintenance of the 4x4 block. While the amount of energy may drop slightly after the first semester, we have found that it levels off after the first year. Teachers and students soon adapt to the new pace and from our experience as trainers and researchers, we found that they prefer the change. Our research indicates a consistent 78–85 percent rate of success. These views come from teachers, students, and parents.

STEP FIVE: EXAMINE TEST SCORE DIFFERENCES

While there is much support for the 4x4 model, there is conflicting evidence of academic improvement using the model. This is especially true for the first and perhaps the second year. Test scores remain about the same in most areas, with higher scores showing improvement in the history and social studies areas. We attribute this improvement to a move away from excessive lecturing and allowing students to become interactive with the learning process through the use of advanced instructional strategies. It is important to state that, at least from the beginning, the purpose of the alternative scheduling models was for other reasons than improving test scores.

STEP SIX: WELCOME THE THIRD YEAR MAGIC

In many professions, employees experience a third year success. It is after the third year that most teachers decide to continue teaching or move to a new career. The same is true in the 4x4: in the third year, the schools get and maintain up to 85 percent effectiveness, as reported in teacher surveys. Students respond similarly as seen in Graph 1. Happiness or acceptance is evident. Teachers are happy with the block. In report after report the most often recorded written response has been, "I would never want to return to a traditional schedule, now that I have taught in a blocked schedule." Also with respect to scores, we notice in most situations, that by the third year we see an increase in test scores. Scores improve because the block provides for a philosophy of improvement. An entire organization of improvement is created. This varies from school to school, but can happen in any school if implementation is carried out correctly.

GRAPH 1. STUDENT PERCEPTION OF 4X4 SUCCESS OVER A THREE-YEAR PERIOD

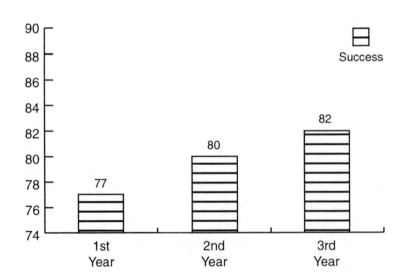

STEP SEVEN: 4X4 BLOCK SCHEDULING MODIFICATIONS FOR THE FUTURE

From our research and training, we recommend that all schools include these items in their planning sessions as they begin or modify the block model.

1. Continue with the block scheduling. Consider developing a procedure for obtaining more feedback from parents on a semester level.

2. Central office personnel need to continue developing system-wide and school-wide training opportunities for teachers in instructional pacing and instructional strategies.

3. Attempts need to be made to continue improving the achievement levels of students during both semesters. To help achieve the greatest academic progress while using the 4x4 model, we believe it would be useful to eliminate the post holiday down time of the exam period, which in effect may have a negative impact on the start of the second semester. Accomplishing this objective requires that the exam period be moved to precede the holidays. (This, in turn, would push the start of the school year back an equivalent period.) This change would have several positive effects:

   a. Down time or wasted time would be eliminated at a critical period of the year.

   b. Students would receive immediate feedback about the quality of their efforts.

   c. Students would be given the opportunity to demonstrate their knowledge while it is fresh in their minds.

   d. Teachers would be able to get a better reading of student progress.

   e. And of greater importance, the system might see steady increase in student test scores.

4. School discipline will continue to be a problem with beginning teachers. Plan a detailed training program for classroom management with newly hired teachers. Make sure that every school has a school safety plan and that every teacher include procedures for operating a safe and disciplined classroom.

5. To help achieve the greatest academic progress in the 4x4 model, we believe it would be useful to modify the course offerings in foreign language in one of two ways:

   a. Hire more language teachers so there would be no great gap in time from the first to second levels of the subject.

   b. Or, a more practical approach may be to block students into a 90-minute period for the entire year and teach the class as an intensive course. The student would thus meet the equirements for the first two levels.

6. Principals should be required to monitor the classrooms during the last 30 minutes of the periods to ensure that teachers are using every possible minute in an instructionally effective manner.

7. We recommend that an administrator's academy be established to help prepare principals acquire greater skills in the areas of curriculum development, instructional implementation, and faculty supervision.

8. In addition to schools being safe and orderly, schools should be made more inviting. The first place where this should happen is in the office environment. We recommend that all receptionists, secretaries, and assistants be placed into a training program that will assist them in becoming more open and inviting to all who visit the office areas.

As we move into the next century and beyond, we must prepare our children with the skills necessary to adapt and survive in a continually changing world and to live in harmony with a great diversity of people. We believe that the best method in which to accomplish this is through a curriculum that is based on a futurist philosophy. We believe also that the 4x4 block model affords the best design for allowing flexibility in instruction that will be required in such a rapidly changing and greatly diverse society. Therefore, we recommend that the following items be included in future models of the block:

1. A required set of courses that espouses a common set of learning for a futurist society;

2. Numerous electives that allow for students to develop individual talents and skills that go beyond the traditional model found in the schools today;

3. New methods and alternatives for testing be created to better measure what students learn in school;

4. AP testing should be scheduled on a semester basis instead of once a year;

5. All first-year teachers are assigned a mentor who has undergone mentor training, and that the mentor work with the beginning teacher for the first three years of the new teacher's career;

6. Business partnerships and exchanges be developed for students, especially students not planning to pursue the traditional, four-year college, post-secondary education;

7. Procedures be standardized for the admissions process into colleges and universities with respect to interpretation of high school course work.

PART III

IMPLEMENTING THE 4x4 BLOCK SCHEDULE

9

REALIGNING THE CURRICULUM FOR 4X4 INSTRUCTION

In their book *Curriculum Development: Theory into Practice,* Daniel and Laurel Tanner (1995) created a list describing three levels at which teachers function. The lowest of these is Level I, which describes teachers and administrators who merely *maintain* the established curriculum. Level II describes those who *refine* the established curriculum. Educators in this group are aware of the need for change and innovation, but fail to go far enough. They still tend to compartmentalize subject areas. Theory and practice continue to remain separate. The final and most desirable position is Level III, which describes those who take an integrated view of curriculum and seek to continually *examine and rework* it in its entirety. They strive to connect theory and practice and frequently consult professional literature for recent educational research.

Tanner and Tanner (1995) are quick to point out that these levels are not a *sequence* of levels. In other words, first-year teachers do not start as Level I teachers and progress to Level III through years of experience. Rather, this list reflects teacher attitudes toward their profession. Ideally, a first-year teacher should start his/her career at Level III, despite lack of experience. Critics maintain that preservice teachers should concern themselves with establishing daily instructional routines. Combining educational theories to these established routines can be done later through professional development and experience. Tanner and Tanner, and John Dewey for that matter, contend that beginning teachers should establish instructional practices that are backed and approved by current research. Teachers, like all humans, are creatures of habit. All too often, routines can become rooted into a teacher's mode of instructing and remain there even after updated professional development shows that the established routine is not educationally sound. Conversely, an educationally sound system that, for whatever reason, is not working with a particular group of students, is just as ineffective as one that is not educationally sound. Therefore, taking the attitude that the curriculum should be in a constant state of evolving ought to be standard fare for the beginning teacher as well as for the more experienced one. Unfortunately, most educators operate at Level I or II and not at Level III.

In the 4x4 block model, it is imperative that teachers examine Levels I, II, and III issues, but often none are reviewed, leaving the textbook or an outline of content as the major guide for instructional direction.

THE PROCESS OF CURRICULUM ALIGNMENT: ESTABLISHING SCOPE, SEQUENCE, AND SCHEDULING

Curriculum alignment is an essential element in the total success of implementing the block. From our experiences, this element is not reviewed by teachers and negatively impacts the amount of content that can be covered in a specific time period. The first three elements in curriculum alignment include scope, sequence, and scheduling. *Scope* tends to be related to the amount of content in the curriculum and what is to be taught in a certain period of time. Educators develop a K–12 perspective curriculum from viewing scope as the basic outcome of what students are to learn in the formal schooling process. In finalizing the program structure, one may examine math, writing, or science programs for specific outcomes related to subject area. In the program part of the scope, the teacher can see what is to be taught in specific grades or courses.

In sequencing, educators examine the order of information or skills that must be taught to achieve the desired outcomes.

For example, in the Language arts program, teachers instruct readiness skills in reading at kindergarten to basic skills in elementary and middle schools to English in the high school. Teachers strive to put content in a meaningful order. Some courses such as mathematics and science are sequential and require a step-by-step approach. In process skills such as observing, comparing, and inferring, there can be a definite order in which higher order process skills are developed. In the sequencing, evident patterns emerge at various levels in the high school. In high school courses, the sequencing becomes extremely important in order to include all of the desired content. Most of the content has been prescribed by the various state departments and the local boards of education. In most states, teachers will find biology being taught in the tenth grade, however in other places it may be taught in the eleventh or the ninth grade. However, the scope of the content is similar. To be educationally sound, there is a sequence of the basic biology class taught before advanced biology and usually before chemistry and physics courses. Once courses have been developed for scope and sequence, scheduling is the next step.

Administrators and curriculum leaders become more involved at this stage. Their role is to make sure that course offerings are presented at a particular time and offered on a regular basis to ensure all students the opportunity to take the classes. Scheduling becomes more important as we move from curriculum alignment to instructional alignment. If the courses are not aligned in the schedule in the right fashion, it will be difficult to implement the desired curriculum.

THE ABC-D PLAN

When realigning the curriculum, teachers can examine three basic models that will prove to be time-wise and will allow for the maximum use of desired content. This is called the ABC-D plan.

A - ABANDONMENT

In the ABC-D plan, the A stands for Abandonment. The concept of abandonment is not new in the curriculum world. In the effective schools research of the 1980s, researchers found that in order succeed in designing an effective school, some part of the content had to be abandoned to allow time to implement the remaining content in an orderly and appropriate fashion. When examining the abandonment model, we refer to this as the prioritizing approach. When analyzing any curricular model, whether it be from the state department, the local board, or even from the textbook alone, teachers begin to plan what to teach in a course. They begin by listing their intended topics, usually in the order they plan to teach. (These usually have a sequence which may be skill-related.) Many are arranged by theme.

What teachers should be striving to do is to eliminate, move, or modify the competencies or guidelines in curriculum. The first step in prioritization is to list or group patterns of concepts, units, or mini-units. The teacher prioritizes these in Table 1 below. In the table, twelve basic groupings of items are presented. (These numbers will be more or less in most cases.) Sometimes we can do a factor analysis on this and break down the content in particular areas. In most cases these are listed in the local curriculum. A goal may be to abandon two or three in the list of twelve. In the block schedule, 10–15 percent of class time will be lost in the course of a year. We find that from our research and observations, teachers using traditional models often fail to use their time effectively and are teaching beyond the prescribed curriculum. In the block, the abandonment model and the use of various instructional models will cause an increase in interactive learning time. For example, one can focus on a total of twelve concepts for the course and decide to abandon two components that could be eliminated from the course. Often this is material that has been added by the teacher over the years. Teachers implement the curriculum and should not add to the curriculum. Simply follow the curriculum for the course and implement in a process of detail. In a case where the curriculum is tightly outlined and the teacher strives to cover all material, he or she may choose one or two areas where similar competencies may be combined and taught simultaneously. For example, the Civil War and the Revolutionary War competencies may be taught together within the concepts of Restoration. In the English classroom, Epic Poetry may be taught as a part of a general Poetry Unit. We recommend that teachers find two or more concepts to abandon or combine with similar items.

TABLE 1

9th Grade English - Abandonment			
Speech	Epic Poems	Film	Advertising
Poetry	Technology	Drama	Short Story
Fiction	Nonfiction	Research	Novel

Notes to Remember:

1. Teachers must not use the abandonment model to cut required content or competencies. The only content that should be abandoned may include superfluous examples, excess content, or information outside of the content area that teachers may have added over the years.

2. Group competencies together that may be taught in one unit instead of separate lessons, such as process skills or English short stories. Two or three short stories will enable students to understand selected literary terms and the general concept of short stories. It is not necessary to inundate them with ten or more short stories.

3. Isolate the strengths and weaknesses of teaching styles, content examples, and student ability. Create recommendations to deal with the weaknesses.

B - BLOCKING

In the second curriculum alignment model the B is referred to as the Blocking plan or the cooperative approach to curriculum alignment. In the blocking model there is a similar pattern that will emerge (as seen in Table 2). Pretend there are twelve blocks of similar items such as units or skills, content, and various situations or classes. In this model the content is blocked and placed in order. Teachers can mark their use as "T" for teacher-directed, "T/S" for teacher- and student-directed, and "S" for students-directed. Most will be teacher-directed, meaning that the teacher plans to include this content within the course. The teacher will be responsible for preparing all the material. There may be an area where teachers and students can share teaching. The teacher could start a basic content, such as pollution, and have students research thermal, water, and air pollution. Learning stations, product or instructional packages, use of contracts, use of library, all are useful to responsible students and also serve as good tools. The teacher provides perimeters and materials. This works well when students work on this over a period of time, alone or with peers. The student is held accountable for the content and the assignments can be completed as cooperative projects. It is our opinion that only 10 percent of the content should ever be taught in a student-directed manner. Another alternative would be to use the T/S, giving teachers more variety and flexibility in selecting contents.

TABLE 2

9th Grade English - Blocking			
Speech	Epic Poems	Film	Advertising
T/S	T	S	S
Poetry	Technology	Drama	Short Story
T	T	T/S	T/S
Fiction	Nonfiction	Research	Novel
T	T	S	T/S

C - CLUSTERING

The C stands for the clustering model. The clustering model is shown in Table 3. The same twelve items are used as in Table 2. This model is known as the thematic approach. The twelve items are clustered into three categories, themes, or patterns, or three basic sections of the course. These three major units may be carried over a long period of time. We recommend this approach over the other two (abandonment and blocking). There is no attempt to remove content. Content is merged into a more meaningful pattern. For example, in U.S. History there could be a grouping of wars. All the content of war can be taught in one long cluster to look for patterns of prewar climate, the political manifestations, causes, restoration, postwar reconstruction. In a master plan or unit on war, timelines should be drawn and

TABLE 3

Cluster of the 12 Original Topics into Three Units	
Unit One: Literature	**Unit Two: Writing/ Presentational Skills**
Fiction - Short Story	Research Paper
Novel	Speech
Nonfiction	
Poetry - Epic Poetry	**Unit Three: Media and Technology**
Drama	Computer Technology
	Advertising
	Film

posted for students to see the sequence of time. To compare the similarities of the various wars, highlight mini-themes or curricular threads, such as politicians, taxation, etc. In an English classroom, a cluster of media and technology could group together computer technology, advertising, and film. The cross correlation between these topics can result in student investigations into advertising on the Internet, in films and in print media. Selecting content is difficult in the beginning; however, this approach is compelling when students see the relevance of what they are learning and how information may be linked. This approach can be implemented to focus on higher-order thinking skills. Weaknesses may occur in not being able to see the chronological order of events.

D - DEVELOPMENT OF A PACING GUIDE

The ABC part of the alignment plan are choices of methodology in realigning the curriculum. This should be done in grade level or content teams. Work together for standardization throughout the school. The D clause, or Development of a course pacing guide, is simply what every teacher develops. Teachers or departments choose an A, B, or C model, which will lead them to the development of D. The pacing guide is derived directly from the prioritization and organization developed in one of the previous models.

THE PROCESS OF INSTRUCTIONAL ALIGNMENT

Once the scope of the course has been determined and the sequence delineated, it is important to move to instructional alignment. The initial step for the classroom teacher when planning instruction is to develop a pacing guide or a listing of planned course topics to be taught in a semester. Pacing guides detail the length of time needed to teach each content cluster and may also include resources, instructional methods, and individual student assignments. Many teachers question the purpose of developing a pacing guide, especially if they have never been involved in long-range planning for past courses. The value of a pacing guide is immeasurable as it aids teachers in making mental and instructional adjustment to a blocked period. The formation and evaluation of pacing guides will further help teachers succeed in the transitory phase and into the first year on the block in several pronounced ways:

1. The adjustment to the class time difference. Pacing guides can help teachers plan for the extended classes so that time is not wasted, but used completely. During the first year on a block, many teachers find that they are not completely successful in effectively utilizing every minute of a blocked period. The pacing guide can help teachers realize that more than one concept may be taught per day and will hopefully encourage effective planning so that the two or three concepts taught in one period are interrelated. The pacing guide will ultimately help teachers prevent the loss of any instructional time and aid them in the organization of their courses.

2. The adjustment to the semester time difference. It is imperative for every teacher to create his or her own personal pacing guide. Teachers from various departments may help one another in the initial development stages, but every teacher has their own unique teaching style. To internalize the time change, the creation of a pacing guide will enable teachers to get a better "feel" of the school year before it begins. Prior to the first year on the block, teachers should create detailed pacing guides and plan complete lessons for the first month of school. Many teachers interviewed by the authors have concluded that they underanticipated the rate they could cover material and the rate their students could learn. Teachers repeatedly reported that they taught the one month of lesson plans in less than two weeks. The creation of a pacing guide should eliminate this problem.

3. The adjustment of effectively using the entire period. Pacing guides can help teachers prevent lesson organizations of 50 minutes of class and 40 minutes of study hall or homework completion. To maximize the effectiveness of the 4x4 block, teachers must use each instructional minute in an effective manner. It would be impossible to cover course material and for students to learn the required content if teachers do not plan on using the entire period. A brisk pace will ensure content coverage, whereas ineffective planning and wasted time will lead to student boredom, and ultimately to lower test scores. The pacing guide focuses teachers and puts them on a clear path as they teach required subject matter in creative and inspiring ways. The wise use of time is a key factor in success on the block.

4. The adjustment in the use of teaching strategies conducive to the blocked class. Pacing guides can aid teachers in the development of strategies appropriate for certain content areas within each course taught. The pacing guide is not a lesson plan; however, it may include a column or a reference to strategies a teacher may use with each content area. As with any planning, these strategies my change during the year depending upon the students' ability level, but it is helpful to begin planning strategies for the entire year. During the first year on the block, teachers build a series of strategies that will work in their content area and assignments related to the strategies. The pacing guide will serve the teacher as a tool in the first step toward planning the individual lessons.

Even after the first semester and then after the first year, teachers will still use pacing guides as a powerful tool in planning effective instruction. Pacing guide use after the first year benefits the teacher in several ways:

1. Abandonment Reexamination: After the course has been taught and students have been tested on their knowledge, teachers can analyze which teaching strategies, content examples, and student assignments were most beneficial and which did not seem to promote learning. Teachers can then select topics, content, strategies, or superfluous examples to abandon from the course and the pacing guide. (Note: Review ABC-D Plan.)

2. Time Considerations: Experience gained from teaching in a block schedule will enable teachers to reexamine the time planned for learning and the actual teaching time of the previous semester or year. Adjustments can then be made to the pacing guide based on the actual time used and the need to delete unnecessary days or add days for various strategies of reinforcement.

3. Course Content Organization: Courses may be organized in units by topics and themes. These units can be designed in a single subject-format, chronologically, correlated with two subjects or more, or integrated based on specific themes. Pacing guide development after the first semester and/or year may include a slow change in course organization depending on the content area. Skill-based courses where students must learn step one before learning step two may not have the same latitude to change course organization, as history, English, and some vocational courses.

STEPS IN DEVELOPING A PACING GUIDE

Step One: List Course Content. When first starting the design of a pacing guide, teachers begin with the specific model of curriculum alignment used previously for organization of the material planned in the course. All content and objectives must be the organizing force in creating the guide. Begin by listing in order the topics, units, or lessons to be taught within the semester. The topics are listed in the order a teacher plans to teach during the semester. Some teachers start from the beginning while others prefer to work from the end and retrace steps to the beginning. This initial organization is completed in a general manner by simply listing the titles of the units to be taught. Beside each unit, cluster, or theme, teachers determine the length of time necessary to teach each section. (See Examples 1 and 2.)

EXAMPLE 1

9th Grade English

Short Story Unit	15 days
Nonfiction Unit	5 days
Poetry Unit	15 days
Drama Unit	15 days
Novel Unit	20 days
Research Paper	10 days
Technology Unit	5 days
Padding Days	5 days
Total Days =	90 days

EXAMPLE 2

Physical Science

I. Chemistry: First Nine Weeks

1. Scientific Method and Measurement	7 days
2. Elements, Compounds and Mixtures	4 days
3. The Atom	5 days
4. Periodic Table and Families	14 days
5. Chemical Reactions	15 days

II. Physics: Second Nine Weeks

1. Motion	5 days
2. Forces	12 days
3. Work, Power and Simple Machines	8 days
4. Heat and Uses	7 days
5. Electricity	8 days
6. Magnetism	5 days
Total Days =	90 days

Step Two: Develop a Daily Pacing Guide. Teachers move into the second step from a listing of topics to creating a daily pacing guide. Using the general list of topics, teachers now organize the specific topics to be taught each day under each unit or topic. (See Examples 3 and 4.) These daily guides need to include objectives, assessment, and resources to be used. A detailed pacing guides will include testing dates and should include three to five days of "padding." The padding days will be used for unanticipated interruptions such as snow days, field trips, assemblies, or anything that removes students out of class and has not been formally planned into the schedule. Padding days can also be used in classes where teachers and students want to be further involved in investigating a topic. Students may become excited about a certain area and want to research

EXAMPLE 3

Algebra I - Week Two

Monday - Scientific Notation
Decimal to Scientific
Scientific to Decimal
Correcting Incorrect Scientific Notation
(Homework: Problems 8-17, pp. 28–29)

Tuesday - Scientific Notation - Multiplying and
Dividing
Absolute Value
(Homework: Problems - Green Worksheet
#12)

Wednesday - Rational vs. Irrational
Review: Rounding Numbers
Additive/Multiplicative Inverses
(Homework: Quiz Review Problems
1–10, p. 35)

Thursday - Quiz # 2
Squares/Radicals/Square Roots
Vocabulary
How to Use the Table
Approximating Square Roots with a
Calculator
(Homework: Problems 1-6, p. 37)

Friday - Review: Prime Factorization
Simplifying Square Roots
Super Math Bingo

or experiment with course material. Teachers cannot allow this to be an everyday occurrence, it may only happen once or twice in a course or semester. The pacing guide is developed to help teachers stay on topic and focused on completing the course

---

EXAMPLE 4

9th Grade English

1 day - Introduction to Course
         Rules/Guidelines/Materials
         Personal Collage - Homework

1 day - Presentation of Personal Collage
         Grouping Effectively
         Listening Activity
         Team Procedures
         Team Roles

13 days - Short Story Unit
         I. Plot (3 days)
              Suspense - Ronald Dahl - "Poison"
              Exposition - Sir Arthur Conan Doyle - "The
              Adventure of the Speckled Band"
         II. Character (2 days)
              Truman Capote - "A Christmas Memory"
              Amado Muro - "Maria Tepache"
         III. Setting (2 days)
              Conflict - James Ramsey Ullman - "Top Man"
              Dorothy M. Johnson - "A Man Called Horse"
         III. Point of View (2 days)
              Jessamyn West - "The Hat"
         IV. Theme (2 days)
              Nicolai Chukovski - "The Bridge"
         V. Irony (2 days)
              James Thurber - "The Little Girl and the Wolf"
                              "The Princess and the Tin Box"
              Guy de Maupassant - "The Necklace"

** HOMEWORK: Short Story Project - Student Application of
Literary Terms.**

content in the most beneficial way possible for students. Another reason for padding days may be for academic difficulties. A class may not understand a concept or may need an extensive review to attain a new skill. This does not necessarily need to take an entire period and should only happen one or two times a year. Another way to use padding is found in the blocking model as the student-centered teaching days may fall on the padding days. Note: It may also be helpful in this step to think back to the traditional year and remember the midpoint of the year or course content taught up to the Christmas holidays. This can now serve as a midpoint in your planning of daily lessons and the time it may take to teach each topic.

Step Three: Develop Assessment and Resource List. Include possible assessment tools in the pacing guide to ensure that a wide variety of learning styles have been met. All students should be tested to discover their individual style or learning strengths. Possible lists of materials could include items such as supplementary novels, handouts, study guides, textbooks, maps, journals, globes, lab equipment, library, people, audiotapes, test banks, word lists, and field trips. Assessment possibilities could include rubrics, individual or group presentations, mini-lessons, reading reports, portfolios, speeches, creative projects, individual conferences, learning contracts, and peer evaluations. (See Examples 5 and 6 which include assessment and resource materials.)

Step Four: Develop a Classroom Management Plan. The time should be planned for review of expectations for classroom behavior. According to the philosophy of the teacher or team, there must be a highly developed classroom management plan that provides boundaries for a safe and orderly environment. Within the classroom there must be rules or procedures for student transitions between activities, verbal interaction among classmates, groups, and with the teacher, and administrative procedures for administrative tasks such as passing up homework, collecting supplies, or passing out materials. Within the plan there should be procedures for any unexpected emergency, such as a student becoming extremely ill (insulin shock, epileptic seizure,

EXAMPLE 5. PACING GUIDE FOR BRITISH ENGLISH LITERATURE

Unit/Topic	Correlation with Local and State Goals and Objectives	Resources Strategies	Classroom Management
Anglo-Saxon Period	Goals 1, 2, 3, and 4	Textbook	Student Credo: "I am Responsible for ALL my ACTIONS."
1. Historical Background	Objectives: Reading 1.1, Writing 1.1, 1.3, 1.5, 2.4, Listening 3.3, and and Speaking 3.1, 4.1	Video on Historical Background	Portfolio Contract Learning
2. Works/ Authors *Beowulf*		Study Guide for *Beowulf* Audio Recording from the Anglo-Saxon translation of *Beowulf*	Parent Conferences
Grendel - poetry		Case Method - Trip to Library Graphic Organizers	
Bede's *History of the English Church and People*			
3. Literary Terms: folk epic, lyric, riddle, satire			

Time Requirements: Two Weeks

EXAMPLE 6. PACING GUIDE FOR EARTH SCIENCE

	1	2	3	4	4
Goals and Objectives	1	2	3	4	4
Days for Completion	1 week	4 days	7 days	3 weeks	
Textbook Chapters and Materials	Ch. 1-3 Video #12	Ch. 8-9	Ch 4-7	Ch. 10 Blue Text Ch. 8	Ch. 12-16
Strategies	Cooperative Groups Computer Labs	Cooperative Groups Computer Labs	Synectics Computer Labs	Inquiry Method Case Method Field Trip Computer Labs	Jurisprudential Inquiry Computer Labs
Key Concepts	Astronomy Geology Meteorology Climatology Oceanography Maps Careers in Earth Science	Mineral, Magma minerals by evaporation and precipitation Properties of Minerals Arrangement of Atoms	Composition of Earth, Lithosphere Mantle, Core Plate Tectonics History, Evidence Mechanisms Anticlines and Synclines Subduction Zones Hot Spots	Igneous Rock Intrusive, Extrusive Sedimentary Rock Examples of Sed. Fossils & Landforms Metamorphic Rocks Examples of Met. Regional and Contact Landforms	Weathering Physical and Chemical Processes: Gravity, Wind, Water, Glacial, Erosion Soil Formation Soil Profiles Effect of People on Erosion
Alternative Assessment	Portfolio Presentation	Portfolio Presentation	Portfolio Individual Project	Portfolio Logs	Portfolio Simulation
Classroom Management	Individualized Contracts, Set of Posted Consequences, Lab Guidelines, Materials Check Lists, Attendance Incentive Program, Parent Contacts and Conferences, and Absence Policy for Makeup Work				

etc.), or from an accident in a chemistry lab or an injury in physical education class. Safe schools are also safe havens for youth. Teachers should have a plan that is a component of the school plan to report any strangers in the building, sexual, verbal, or physical harassment of students, or suspected child abuse or neglect. Students will follow these guidelines in the classroom and outside the classroom.

Step Five: Plan Activities for Each Instructional Day. When planning activities in a pacing guide, they should remain general. The activities will be planned in great detail in the teacher's daily lesson plans. Short names representing activities need to be included in the guides for each day. Examples may include synectics, cooperative grouping, Socratic seminars, etc. Simply listing these short names for activities will aid in planning to meet individual learning styles and in creating a variety of activities of high interest. (See Examples 5 and 6.)

FIRST-YEAR SUCCESS AND PACING GUIDES

Pacing guides during the first year are important for beginning and experienced teachers alike as it helps to make the pace brisk and efficient. First-year teachers and any teacher moving to the block during the first year must check the pacing guide constantly to ensure coverage of course content. The pacing guide must be reviewed each day and modified when necessary. After the first semester on a block, pacing guides usually undergo a comprehensive examination for the effective use of time, student achievement and appropriateness of the lessons. Modifications after the first semester and the first year will result in positive, future pacing. The modifications often remedy the difference between the anticipated course and what actually occurs while teaching the course. Sometimes material is taught at a greater speed than ever before or teachers may find that there are areas where they predicted the lesson would take one week and it actually took a week and three days. Pacing guides will change, as seen in Examples 7 and 8.

EXAMPLE 7. CHANGES IN AMERICAN HISTORY PACING GUIDE

Original American History Guide Unit Three - Civil War	Revised American History Guide Unit Three - Civil War
1 day - Secession of the Southern States Introduction to Unit - Lecture	1 day - Causes of the War Webbing Activity Create Bulletin Board
2 days - Abraham Lincoln Video	1 day - Abraham Lincoln Video - Response Groups
1 day - Emancipation Proclamation Video	1 day - Emancipation Proclamation Audio Tape and Jigsaw II Study
6 days - Important Battles Chronological Study Lecture - Graphic Organizer Create Timeline	6 days - Important Battles Case Study 1 - Assign Research Roles 2 - Research and Contract Formation 3 - Lecture - Create Timeline 4 - Individual Presentations 5 - Socratic Seminar - Last Year of the War
2 days - Last Year of the War	
1 day - Results of the War	1 day - Results of the War Graphic Organizer - Cause and Effect
1 day - Death of Lincoln	1 day - Death of Lincoln
1 day - Test	1 day - Test and Intro to Unit Four
15 Total Days	12 Total Days

EXAMPLE 8. CHANGES IN ART III PACING GUIDE

Original Art III Pacing Guide

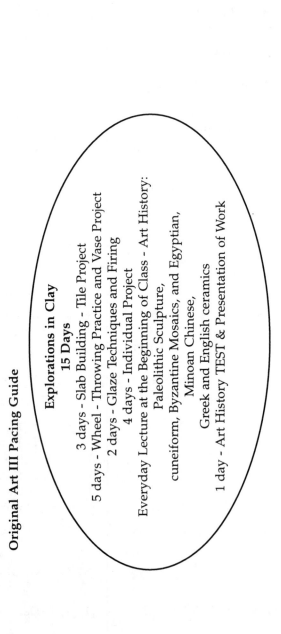

Explorations in Clay
15 Days

3 days - Slab Building - Tile Project
5 days - Wheel - Throwing Practice and Vase Project
2 days - Glaze Techniques and Firing
4 days - Individual Project
Everyday Lecture at the Beginning of Class - Art History:
Paleolithic Sculpture,
cuneiform, Byzantine Mosaics, and Egyptian,
Minoan Chinese,
Greek and English ceramics
1 day - Art History TEST & Presentation of Work

Revised Art III Pacing Guide

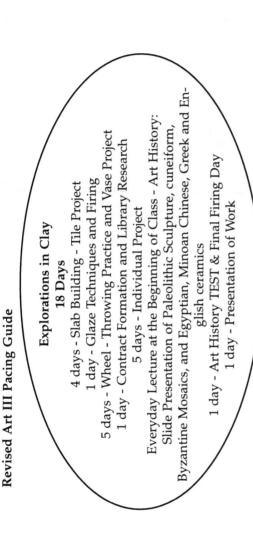

Explorations in Clay
18 Days

4 days - Slab Building - Tile Project
1 day - Glaze Techniques and Firing
5 days - Wheel - Throwing Practice and Vase Project
1 day - Contract Formation and Library Research
5 days - Individual Project
Everyday Lecture at the Beginning of Class - Art History:
Slide Presentation of Paleolithic Sculpture, cuneiform,
Byzantine Mosaics, and Egyptian, Minoan Chinese, Greek and English ceramics
1 day - Art History TEST & Final Firing Day
1 day - Presentation of Work

Materials: 50 bags of clay - earthenware, white; kiln; 4 wheels; slab roller, slide projector; cone 04 glazes; plastic; clay tools - 20 sets; student contract forms; kiln and wheel schedule; bats and shelf tags

Preparation for Individual Project Show
1 - Notify local library of show dates and reserve upper gallery space.
2 - Sign contracts with students for individual projects after third day of unit. Determine criteria for displaying work in the public library show prior to completion of contracts.
3 - Create kiln and wheel schedule for class and after school work.
4 - Upon presentation of work, students display work in school gallery. Fifteen pieces go to public library for annual Expressions in Clay show.

The following blank guides may be used to help teachers list course content and begin to think about course organization, time, activities, and resources.

PACING GUIDE			
School: Teacher:			
Course Title: Textbooks:			
School Year: Exam Date:			
Date	Goal/Objective	Topic	Textbook Page

Weekly Pacing Guide			
Course:		Date:	
Monday Time	Topic	Textbook Pages Resources	Strategies
Tuesday Time	Topic	Textbook Pages Resources	Strategies
Wednesday Time	Topic	Textbook Pages Resources	Strategies
Thursday Time	Topic	Textbook Pages Resources	Strategies
Friday Time	Topic	Textbook Pages Resources	Strategies

CONTENT-SPECIFIC NEEDS

In the vocational area, pacing guides need to include student travel time to businesses or vocational centers. For art classes, materials and supplies should be listed in detail. The materials needed may increase, so make sure you effectively plan for the use of materials. Many schools have experienced a 35-50 percent increase in material needs and copy needs. In the English department, pacing needs often involve the sharing of novels between teachers. It is important to indicate in guides and plan for other materials that must be shared. In the science or math classes teachers need to plan together for lab space and materials that must be shared. In band and chorus, plan for competitions, fund raisers, performances, and booster meetings.

In physical education, location is often important to plan. The students may spend a week in a regular classroom for health and then several days on the baseball field, several days in the gymnasium, and several days in the weight room. Physical education teachers may also plan to take their students to local golf courses or bowling alleys during the period.

It is imperative that every teacher develop his or her own pacing guide. It may be effective for teachers of the same subject to work together as a team in this development, however, it is valuable for each teacher to have a personal pacing guide. These guides should be revised after the first semester. As teachers see the guides needing adjustment, modification can be made during the semester. The reason it is so valuable for teachers to develop their own guides is that teachers teach at different paces. Each teacher's style of delivering instruction is different. Teachers may also have the same content and various academic levels in their classes. Various periods may be interrupted because of a split lunch or other modified block plan.

EVALUATING PACING GUIDES

Step One: Modification During the Course. Immediate knowledge of changing days or need for adjustment may result from incorrect prediction of time allotment. Adjustments may also need to be made during the school year for cultural differences, academic expectations, or difficulty levels based on ability.

Step Two: Modification at the End of the First Semester. Evaluation of entire course should involve assessment of time spent in each content cluster or grouping and the effectiveness of the activities used to teach the content. Did the activities help students or hinder their learning? Examination of the use of time should also include a search for wasted time and modifications to eliminate or abandon superfluous material.

Step Three: Modification at the End of the First Year. After an entire year's experience, teachers can alter the pacing guide to maintain greater reliability for effectiveness. These guides may still change from year to year, depending on the students involved and the required course content.

Once the guide has been established it is time for teachers to move on to developing lesson plans. (Chapter 10.) Aligning instruction is the last phase of planning that teachers must complete for a successful foray into block scheduling.

REFERENCES

Tanner, D., & Tanner, L. (1995). *Curriculum theory into practice.* Columbus: Merrill.

10

LESSON DESIGN AND INSTRUCTIONAL STRATEGIES

When aligning instruction in the 4x4, it is necessary to begin by developing units or major concept clusters for instruction. The development of pacing guides must be completed prior to the formation of these units. Pacing guides should list, by day, the topics to be covered, the activities to be used, and the classroom management details to be enforced throughout the semester. When the lesson is developed, it must be written with more detail than the pacing guide. The lesson plan in a 4x4 can include ideas for transition, moving between activities, differentiation of instruction, meeting the needs of various types of learners, and alternative forms of assessment to gage learning. Lesson plans may also include interdisciplinary designs, which make learning interactive and relevant.

The lesson design for a 4x4 blocked class is usually made up of several activities which are connected in one period. The necessity for multiple activities in various presentational modes during one class period stems from research in effective teaching models and the need to maintain student interest. In a blocked period, students suffer if relegated to one lesson or activity per the usual 90-minute class. Negative classroom behaviors are negligible if the pacing of instruction is brisk and engaging. The lesson must be planned in detail to aid teachers as they move between various activities every 15 to 20 minutes. The structure of the lesson plan may change from class to class or from department to department as teachers plan appropriate content for each course. A teacher may change the structure of a single class from an introductory lecture of 20 minutes rather than 15 minutes, or the teacher may decide to place direct instruction or lecture in the middle of the period for 10 minutes, and then hold a concluding lecture of 10 minutes. Lecture is a highly effective mode for presenting a large amount of content during short periods of time. It may be utilized in numerous ways in the block; however, it should never be overused or delivered in spans of time longer than 20–25 minutes. The type of students being taught is also another factor which may change the time variable in moving from activity to activity. An advanced class may be able to actively listen to a lecture for 30 minutes while a lower-level class may only be able to focus on a lecture for 15 minutes. See Examples 1 and 2 for sample lesson plans showing activity changes.

USE OF VARIED INSTRUCTIONAL STRATEGIES

Varied instructional strategies enable the student in a blocked class to learn on many different levels. In past surveys we have taken, students have reported that one of the things they most liked about the block was the way their teachers taught. Students reported a drop in lecture and an increase in more hands-on activities. Before moving to a block, the chief concern students had about blocked classes was the fear of becoming bored. To maintain high levels of interest and address learning styles, teachers must plan detailed lessons which may include demonstrations, discussions, cooperative learning, the synectics model, case method, inquiry method, and other high-interest models.

TRADITIONAL APPROACHES MODIFIED FOR THE 4X4 BLOCK

Traditional methods included are the lecture, teacher directed discussion and discovery strategies. These have been the major teaching techniques that teachers have used in traditional schedules as well as the 4x4 block schedule. We have taken the three models and placed them in the text for easy comparison. (See

EXAMPLE 1. SAMPLE ACTIVITY CHANGES IN A TYPICAL CHEMISTRY CLASS

Chemistry

10 Min	Warm-up Activity (5 Min.) Homework Problems (10 Min.)
10 Min.	LECTURE: Balancing Equations (15 Min.)
10 Min.	
10 Min	Synectics Activity (50 Min.) Step One - List qualities
10 Min	Step Two - List similarities between Balancing Equations and Building a House
10 Min	Step Three - Personal Analogy - Students become an equation
10 Min	Step Four - Developing a New Analogy
10 Min	Step Five - Students create visual representation of new analogy
10 Min	Review Concepts and Vocabulary Terms (5 Min.) Homework Assignment and Closing (5 Min.)

EXAMPLE 2. SAMPLE ACTIVITY CHANGES IN A TYPICAL HISTORY CLASS

History

10 Min.	Lesson Introduction - Lecture (10 Min.)
10 Min	Cooperative Learning - Jigsaw II Activity - Vietnam Introduction to Activity - Distribute Articles (10 Min.)
10 Min.	Divide into Expert Groups - Read and Complete Article Study (20 Min.)
10 Min	
10 Min	Divide into Share Groups and Teach Peers (15 Min.)
10 Min	Class Discussion (15 Min.)
10 Min.	
10 Min	Writing Response - Students Write Vietnam Story - Topics Handout (15 Min.)
10 Min	Review and Homework Assignment (5 Min.)

Tables 1, 2, and 3.) The first two models are teacher directed and place much of the responsibility upon the instructor to ensure that learning has taken place. In the modified forms with appropriate time limits, lecture and teacher directed instruction can be used effectively. Just stay in the recommended time frames. The discovery model is often used by more creative teachers. Teachers using this method must have excellent questioning skills and ability to motivate the students. Teachers in our modified approach, should focus strongly upon higher-order, problem-solving skills.

NONTRADITIONAL APPROACHES MODIFIED FOR THE 4X4 BLOCK

The traditional approaches presented in the charts include simulations and games, the synectics strategy, the case study method and the cooperative learning strategies. (See Tables 4, 5, 6, and 7.) All four of these models are learner centered. Grouping patterns can vary from individual to large groups, the focus can remain the same. Teachers using these modified versions must be learner centered, creative, guide students to deal with abstractions and be great managers of student behavior. While in most cases, students will become actively engaged in these strategies, a few might lack the responsibility to remain on task appropriately. Individual contracts for managed student assignments work well in some of these cases.

Later in the chapter we have included activities within several subject areas to demonstrate how many of these modified strategies can work effectively. The discussion on case method describes how many of our modified traditional and nontraditonal strategies work within this major style of teaching.

Educators have long assumed that creativity was an innate characteristic that one was either born with or would never posses. William Gordon, designer of synectics, believes that creativity can be enhanced, developed and, perhaps, even learned. Teachers using synectics as a teaching model bring about a metamorphoses in teaching that de-emphasizes rote learning and focuses instead on students' prior knowledge, provoking original creative thought and enhancing retention of content simultaneously.

TABLE 1. TRADITIONAL APPROACHES MODIFIED FOR THE 4X4 BLOCK

	Major Components	Grouping Patterns	Instructional Effectiveness
The Lecture Strategy	◆ Teacher Centered ◆ Direct Instruction Oriented ◆ Review ◆ Advanced Organizers ◆ Objective ◆ Student Practice ◆ Summary	◆ Whole Class ◆ Large Groups ◆ Small Groups	◆ Must be Well Planned ◆ Should Not Exceed 20 Minutes ◆ Introduction to New Content ◆ Focused Outcome ◆ Factual Knowledge ◆ Motivation ◆ Improved With Visuals
	Teaching Skills	**Student Readiness**	**Student Assessment**
	◆ Excellent Speaker ◆ Organizing Lecture Material ◆ Animated - Voice Variations ◆ Involving Students ◆ Checking for Understanding	◆ Must be Taught to Take Notes ◆ Notetaking Must be Monitored Frequently by Teacher	◆ Objective Test ◆ Essay Exams

TABLE 2. TRADITIONAL APPROACHES MODIFIED FOR THE 4X4 BLOCK

	Major Components	Grouping Patterns	Instructional Effectiveness
Teacher Directed Discussion	◆ Teacher Directed ◆ Review/Background Information ◆ Objective ◆ Selection of Topic ◆ Establishing Procedure ◆ Student Practice ◆ Summary	◆ Whole Class ◆ Large Groups ◆ Small Groups (12 to 15 students)	◆ Must be Well Planned ◆ 30-45 Minutes in Length ◆ Focused Outcome ◆ Convergent Topoics ◆ Divergent Topics
	Teaching Skills	**Student Readiness**	**Student Assessment**
	◆ Controlling Participation and Managing Student Behavior ◆ Questioning Strategies ◆ Attention/Motivation ◆ Modifying Pace ◆ Checking for Understanding	◆ Attentive ◆ Willingness to Participate	◆ Objective Test ◆ Essay Exams ◆ Class Presentation

TABLE 3. TRADITIONAL APPROACHES MODIFIED FOR THE 4x4 BLOCK

	Major Components	Grouping Patterns	Instructional Effectiveness
The Discovery Strategy	• Learner Centered • Brainstorming • Selection of a Problem • Selection of Topic • Hypotheses Formation • Student Practice • Conclusion	• Whole Class • Large Groups • Learning Stations • Individual	• Divergent Oriented • 45-60 Minutes in Length • Independent Problem-Solving Which Increases Curiosity • Higher-Order Thinking Skills • Abstractions
	Teaching Skills	**Student Readiness**	**Student Assessment**
	• Questioning Strategies • Organization • Facilitator • Management of Student Behavior • Monitoring for on Task Behavior	• Compare/Contrast • Motivated • Ability to Work in Small Groups • Ability to Work Individually • Remain on Task	• Large Group Discussion • Small Group Discussion • Debriefing Activity • Application/Problem-Solving • Model Building

Table 4. Nontraditional Approaches Modified for the 4x4 Block

	Major Components	Grouping Patterns	Instructional Effectiveness
	◆ Learner Centered ◆ Content Objective ◆ Process Objective ◆ Role Assignment ◆ Rules and Procedures ◆ Conclusion ◆ Resources	◆ Small Groups ◆ Computer Activity ◆ Learning Stations ◆ Individual	◆ Practice Reality ◆ Problem-Solving ◆ Higher-Order Thinking Skills ◆ Introduction to New Concepts ◆ Understanding Social Conflict ◆ Analyzing and Evaluation ◆ Roles Defined
Simulations and Games	**Teaching Skills** ◆ Questioning Strategies ◆ Controlling Participation ◆ Facilitator - Organization ◆ Management of Student Behavior ◆ Checking for Understanding	**Student Readiness** ◆ Ability to be Involved ◆ Motivated ◆ Ability to Work in Small Groups ◆ Ability to Work in Pairs or Individually	**Student Assessment** ◆ Completion of the Simulation ◆ Demonstrations ◆ Class Presentation ◆ Creativity

TABLE 5. NONTRADITIONAL APPROACHES MODIFIED FOR THE 4X4 BLOCK

	Major Components	Grouping Patterns	Instructional Effectiveness
The Synetics Strategy	◆ Learner Centered ◆ Selecting Appropriate Concepts ◆ Review ◆ Developing Analogies -Direct Analogies -Personal Analogies -Conflict and Contrast -New Analogies ◆ Organization and Procedures	◆ Small Groups ◆ Large Groups ◆ Individual	◆ Introduction of New Concept ◆ Reviewing Previously Learned Concepts ◆ Analysis ◆ Synthesis ◆ Clarifying Content ◆ Higher-Order Thinking

	Teaching Skills	Student Readiness	Student Assessment
	◆ Questioning Strategies ◆ Controlling Participation ◆ Facilitator - Organization ◆ Management of Student Behavior ◆ Checking for Understanding	◆ Ability to be Involved ◆ Motivated ◆ Ability to Work in Groups ◆ Serious ◆ Open Minded	◆ Creating Analogies ◆ Objective Tests ◆ Standardized Tests ◆ Creativity ◆ Class Discussions

TABLE 6. NONTRADITIONAL APPROACHES MODIFIED FOR THE 4X4 BLOCK

	Major Components	Grouping Patterns	Instructional Effectiveness
The Case Study Method	◆ Learner Centered ◆ Goals and Objectives ◆ Presentation of the Case ◆ Exploration of the Case ◆ Manipulation of Content ◆ Integration ◆ Presentation	◆ Small Groups ◆ Individual	◆ Inductive Reasoning ◆ 60-90 Periods Extended Over Several Days ◆ Group/Individual Investigations ◆ Problem Solving ◆ Higher-Order Thinking
	Teaching Skills	**Student Readiness**	**Student Assessment**
	◆ Questioning Strategies ◆ Controlling Participation ◆ Facilitator - Organization ◆ Management of Student Behavior ◆ Case Assessment	◆ Reference Skills ◆ Motivated ◆ Ability to Work in Small Groups ◆ Team Player ◆ Accept Individual Responsibility for Specific Assignments	◆ Group Presentations ◆ Individual Involvement - Projects ◆ Field Study ◆ Portfolios ◆ Written Presentations

TABLE 7. NONTRADITIONAL APPROACHES MODIFIED FOR THE 4x4 BLOCK

	Major Components	Grouping Patterns	Instructional Effectiveness

Cooperative Learning Strategy	◆ Learner Centered
	◆ Team Building - Team Activity
	◆ Group Goals
	◆ Variety of Organizational Patterns
	  - STAD
	  - Jigsaw II
	◆ Group Presentations
		◆ Pairs
		◆ Triads
		◆ Small Groups
			◆ Inductive Reasoning
			◆ 60-90 Periods Extended Over Several Days
			◆ Group Investigations
			◆ Problem Solving
			◆ Higher-Order Thinking
			◆ Group Practice

	Teaching Skills	**Student Readiness**	**Student Assessment**
	◆ Monitoring ◆ Supportive ◆ Organizational Skills ◆ Management of Student Behavior ◆ Guide	◆ Role Assignment ◆ Role Expectation ◆ Motivated ◆ Team Player ◆ Reference Skills	◆ Group Presentations ◆ Multimedia Projects ◆ Group Assessment ◆ Individual Portfolios

Synectics was originally designed in the 1960s as a method for businesses to group employees according to their thought processes. Educators have been expanded to the synectics model to be used with students in a variety of classroom settings. The use of synectics was initially reserved as a tool for problem-solving, but the approach has become increasingly popular in many instructional areas. Synectics has been used in a variety of settings successfully from the typical classroom to resource rooms for remediation and to academically gifted classes. Currently, synectics is most commonly used with students in middle and high school classrooms.

The synectics model taps the students' creativity through the use of analogies to generate original ideas. Originally, the method revolved around three major steps; direct analogy, personal analogy, and compressed conflict. Actually there are several versions of the model. We have presented the two major versions below. Each of the steps are presented in the following section.

Steps in the Synectics Strategy: Version I

Step One: Direct Analogy
Teacher Responsibilities:
- State analogy for concept
- Assist students in finding
  connections between
  analogy and concept

Student Responsibilities:
- Describe analogy
- Identify connections
  between analogy and
  concept

Step Three: Contrast
Teacher Responsibilities:
- Briefly aid students to
  identify differences
  between the concept and
  the analogy.
Student Responsibilities:
- Identify differences

Step Two: Personal Analogy
Teacher Responsibilities:
- Prompt students to
  become analogy by using
  role-play and examples
- Help students to find
  further connections

Student Responsibilities:
- Describe how it feels to be
  the analogy
- Role-play and write
  using "I" statements

Step Four: New Analogy
Teacher Responsibilities:
- Prompt students to create
  their own analogy

Student Responsibilities:
- Form new analogy
- Explain new analogy

Steps in the Synectics Strategy: Version II

Synectics: Steps in Using Version II

Step One: **Stretching**. Before announcing the topic, the teacher or a student should initiate a short period of mental stretching. A topic should be introduced to the class and students respond with analogies. Researchers have proven the synectics session to be more productive if a warm-up session precedes the actual lesson. .

Step Two: **Introduction**. The teacher introduces a topic to discuss, write about, or a problem to solve to the students. The students think about the topic, brainstorm a few moments, and give a verbal or written description of the topic as it is perceived by them. If the responses are oral, the teacher makes a list of them on the board asking students to provide reasons for their description.

Step Three: **Personal Analogy**. This step is the first of the three core steps created by Gordon and his associates. After the students have described the topic, the teacher asks them to empathize with the subject whether it be living or non-living. By stepping outside one's self and "becoming" the object or idea, the student uses his/her emotions as well as his/her intellect. "I" statements are encouraged during all analogy phases.

Step Four: **Direct Analogy**. Direct analogy requires the student to compare two ideas, topics or objects, transferring the circumstances surrounding one thing to another. In this phase, the student may state something they have seen in another setting and relate it to the current topic, thus introducing an original idea or solution. Direct analogy successfully enhances students' problem-solving and decision-making abilities and opens the door to creative solutions.

Step Five: **Compressed Conflict**. Compressed conflict challenges the student to generate a two-word description of the subject, idea or object in which the two words are opposites. By choosing two opposite descriptive words, it broadens the students' perspective and increases mental flexibility. An example of a compressed conflict analogy would be "deafening silence".

Step Six: **Create a New Analogy**. This requires the students to go back to step four and create a direct analogy that describes compressed conflict words.

Step Seven: **Revisit the Original Topic**. This is the step where the crux of the discussion begins, the student writes the paper, or the problem is solved. A student may choose to utilize all or a portion of the analogies listed in the above process. By opening the students' imaginations, writing becomes more creative and ideas are often original.

In addition to the three core steps of analogies, Gordon has created two teaching strategies for the classroom. One strategy is "Creating Something New" that requires divergent thinking processes by students, using analogies to make something familiar strange. Often, when we are familiar with a subject, the obvious is overlooked and certain characteristics are taken for granted. "Creating Something New" encourages looking at the topic from a different viewpoint enabling students to appreciate all its characteristics. The teacher states a topic and the students suggest analogies restating the topic. Students then make analogies to objects that are not related to the initial subject. When students "make" the familiar strange, they view the problem more objectively and get a deeper insight into the subject. This method is imaginative and promotes creativity.

The second teaching strategy created by Gordon is "Making the Strange Familiar" which requires convergent thinking as the students view a topic that is unfamiliar and make analogies to personalize their concepts. This method is similar to "Creating Something New" except the process is reversed going from the unfamiliar to familiar. "Making the Strange Familiar" promotes analyses on unfamiliar topics through creative thinking.

Many educators have a changed viewpoint today of what should occur in the classroom. Synectics is a method that coincides with the desires of today's educators. Synectics allows the teacher to be the lesson facilitator requiring students to take responsibility for their own learning. Rewards from synectics are intrinsic and are a source of pride for the students. Students are aware of their abilities and do not need extrinsic rewards to tell them they have achieved.

Most educators today believe the school should be an environment that encourages students to take risks. Synectics provides this environment. The teacher facilitates the lesson only. All responses are accepted by the teachers and peers without judgment. Students can feel free to explore new ideas without the threat of criticism or ridicule.

When using the synectics method, it is important that this is an exercise in creativity. Do not allow the students to stop making analogies and return to the original topic too soon. Let the creative ideas flow as long as necessary to develop a good foundation on the topic. Also, synectics can be used in a whole class setting, but small groups tend to be more effective and efficient.

In addition to the benefits of synectics discussed above, synectics helps build camaraderie among students. Because no judgment is placed upon the responses given, students begin to respect one another as equals and creative individuals.

Traditionally, student learning is most often measured by testing. Teachers ask questions that are tangible, structured and can be administered within a limited time period. As such, these questions usually tap into a limited amount of knowledge and skills. It is important for educators to remember that paper and pencil testing is only one way to collect information about student learning. If teachers use different assessments, they can examine a wider range of student abilities often missed by traditional standardized testing. In fact, the exclusive use of non-referenced, standardized tests in making instructional decisions has limitations. As a result, a changing philosophy toward learning and learners has occurred and alternatives to norm-referenced testing have been proposed (Pike & Salend, 1995, p. 15). Effective authentic or performance assessment strategies can help educators and students make sound educational decisions that focuses on student ability, not test scores. The case study method is a technique that focuses on such student ability, not disability. Performance assessment, such as the case study method, is often challenging, but is possibly the best assessment strategy for our students today.

Many schools are designing and using innovative assessment strategies. Some of these are called authentic assessment, performance-based assessment or process assessment. Regardless of the label, each of these techniques has moved beyond the concept of measuring student learning using multiple choice and other simple tests. These relatively new strategies view assessment as a process, not as a single measurement of student learning at one point in time.

The above labels refer to a variety of informal and formal student-centered strategies for collecting and recording information about students. Authentic assessment practices seek to facilitate student learning by linking assessment and instruction procedures that emphasize both the process and products of learning (Pike & Salend, 1995, p. 19).

Case studies are special cases of the problem-solving technique in which students study individual cases representative of a type of institution, issue, problem situation or the like in order to draw conclusions about the type as a whole. Textbook preparations are often insufficient for students to take an in-depth and reflective look at the way they think and respond to a variety of real-life situations. Case studies offer opportunities to deal with specific diversity issues in the classroom such as prejudice, gender bias, poverty and cultural misunderstandings. By acknowledging student's previous experiences and attitudes in response to multicultural and diversity issues, the teacher gains a clearer picture of strategies to use to introduce and integrate additional information and heighten cultural awareness. Anytime an individual is faced with a perplexing situation or a situation where it is necessary to decide what to believe or do, higher order thinking is necessary. This process also promotes and advances students' ethical and moral reasoning. Meaningful teaming occurs when a learner has a knowledge base that can be used with fluency to make sense of the world, solve problems and make decisions. (Lewis & Smith, 1993, p. 42).

An additional benefit of using the case study method is its responsiveness to the varying developmental differences of students (Sudzina, 1993, p. 4). There are a variety of differences in today's classrooms. Developmental and emotional differences are just a couple. The case study method is responsive to all student reflections and opinions.

Student performance can be assessed in many ways using the case study method. Assessment is part of a process that enables students to become successful learners. In this way, assessment becomes the feedback that enables students to be strategic in their own teaming process and enables teachers to adapt the process to meet the needs of their students.

It is important for teachers, prior to assigning case studies, to discuss evaluation procedures with their students. Teachers should prepare students before lessons so that they will have a clear understanding of the teacher's expectations. If students are going to be tested on their grasp of the concepts discussed in a case study, they need to know. Ground rules are a necessity. Teachers may choose to let students set their own goals and work to meet them. Goal setting requires both creative and critical thought, as well as, a sense of evaluation of what is important and what is not. Goal setting also requires time management and an organization of ways to assess whether the goals have been met at the end of the assignment (Parsons & Smith, 1993, p. 21).

When using the case study method, teachers should participate in extensive note-taking to describe a series of events and focus on the activities of one student or a group of students. Interpretation is inevitable, but "rich" description is the ultimate goal (Ennis, 1993, p. 185).

After selecting a topic for study and materials, students can be divided into groups or pairs. Ground rules must be established. The teacher must clearly state the case, so students will not be confused during the lesson. If cases have been previously assigned, it is a good idea to briefly summarize the facts of the case for the benefit of those who may not have prepared. Teachers then should emphasize the importance of reasoning during the assignment, not so much as the solution of the case. Once students begin discussing the case, teachers should remain silent so he/she doesn't give his/her conclusions or opinions. The teacher's role is to pose questions, draw out incomplete answers and to probe inconsistencies (McBumey, 1995, p. 37). So often, students will become anxious and sometimes dispirited when a teacher refuses to tell them the right answer. The case study method is designed to teach students that there is no one right answer.

When using the case study method, student performance can be assessed in many different ways. One technique involves having each individual student present their cases orally to their peers, leading a class discussion incorporating alternative viewpoints. Each student chooses a case from a pre-selected list to present to the class for analysis and discussion (Sudzina, 1993, p. 5). Students are required to complete a written analysis of the case. They are assessed on their oral presentation and written analysis of the case. Role playing, using a panel and symposia are also effective techniques when using case studies.

Rubrics have been used as a scoring instrument for evaluating writing skills. It has only been recently used to evaluate classroom discussions. Teachers can use rubrics to assess each participant's conversational abilities, demonstrated mental and behavioral processes in a group discussion, for a specified amount of time (Frasier, 1997, p. 38). Students are divided into groups or pairs and assigned a case. During this time, the rest of the class is either silently observing the discussion or actually scoring the participants with the same rubric their teacher will use. Groups are designed to foster and reinforce principles of cooperative learning, an effective group strategy that incorporates the benefits of individual accountability and group interdependence (Sudzina, 1993, p. 7).

Teachers assign cases in advance, giving students an opportunity to prepare how the case will be discussed. Students also receive a copy of the checklist used for scoring. After the discussion, teachers often engage in a general class discussion in order to process the groups' perceptions of the case study. Using a checklist, teachers (and students) score each participant and provides individual feedback for them. Students are scored in making inferences, analogies, stating a position, recognizing contradictions, active listening, etc. Points can be taken away for students performing negative behaviors, such as; interrupting, repeating, personal attacks, remaining silent, etc.

Another performance assessment tool that can be used with the case study method is assigning a major research project. Students use a specific case study throughout the course of a semester. At the end of the semester, students present a research paper detailing their analysis of the data they have collected regarding their specific cases. Collected data provides opportunities for description, explanation and understanding about not only what is occurring, but what it means (McConnelly & Wilcox,

1991, p. 7). Students use a variety of sources such as interviews, observations and surveys. Students are evaluated on their final product, a research paper.

Self-evaluation is also an effective assessment tool when using the case study method. Teachers should offer instruction and provide students with numerous opportunities to engage in self-evaluation. Teachers can have students engage in self-evaluation through the use of journals or learning logs. Students can write comments in their logs regarding what they learned using the case study and how they learned (Pike & Salend, 1995, p. 18). Teachers can also obtain information on student attitudes and case study learning by asking students to record responses in their journals to the following examples: The things I liked about the case . . . The things I didn't like about studying the case . . . The things I knew previously about the case . . . (Pike & Salend, 1995, p. 18).

Instead of using traditional testing evaluations, teachers can create a checklist or rubric for individual and/or class discussions, have students prepare a written analysis or research paper and use student self-assessment techniques. These are all highly effective performance assessments using the case study method. These, and other creative methods for the development of higher order thinking, can be challenging for the teacher. But they are a necessity for our learners today and in the future.

When we consider many of our children today will be working at jobs that do not currently exist and that the technological explosion that is currently upon us means that today's knowledge is going to quickly become outdated. The standardized testing methods that are pounded in the minds of today's children will be of no use to them in the future. Students need to know how to learn and how to think critically about information that changes at a rapid rate. We need to give today's students the opportunity to think, grow and make decisions. Students must know how to weigh alternatives and defend their choices. Our classrooms' should be an arena for students to discuss decision-making strategies regarding real-life issues.

Student assessment should move from multiple-choice, short answer, fill-in-the-blank questions to questions that measure higher order thinking. The call for educational accountability throughout the country has had a great impact on the assessment practices in public schools today. Standardized testing is the product of educational accountability.

TECHNOLOGICAL APPROACHES MODIFIED FOR THE 4X4 BLOCK

Teachers are experimenting with the use of technology. Many are beginning to venture out of the word processing mode to allow students to become more involved in the way they desire to study and research for new learnings. Additionally, many teachers are using power point slide presentations and hyperstudio to enhance and modernize their system of instruction. Of greater importance, a few extremely innovative educators are attempting to allow students to use the above tools in addition to other advancement such as the Internet, Distant Learning and the world-wide web to use in presentations, small group student directed instruction. The possibilities with technology are becoming limitless. (See Table 8.)

EXAMPLES OF 4X4 LESSON PLANS

Often teachers in the 4x4 develop layered lessons which they find to be highly effective if students are guided to become involved in a circuit of activities or a series of activities over several days. In a layered lesson plan, students will be participating in several activities on a rotating basis. The planning involved in creating these lesson plans is highly detailed as student movement and individual progress must be constantly evaluated and monitored. The layered lesson plan involves interactive teaching and student-driven learning.

In the following examples, the strategies are shown in developed lessons and layered lessons. These lessons serve to show the use of the 90-minute period, the content of a lesson plan, and the steps used in the previously listed teaching strategies. These strategies can be applied to any course and modified to stress differing course content. Teachers should use these examples as generators for their own classes.

TABLE 8. NONTRADITIONAL APPROACHES MODIFIED FOR THE 4X4 BLOCK

	Major Components	Grouping Patterns	Instructional Effectiveness

The Technology Approach	◆ Learner Centered
	◆ Objective Formation
	◆ Selection of Content
	◆ Selection of Media
	◆ Flexible
	◆ Multisensory
		◆ Small Groups
		  - Pairs
		  - Triads
		◆ Learning Station
		◆ Computer
			◆ Introducing Material
			◆ Simple Facts to Higher-Order Thinking Skills
			◆ Improved Test Scores

	Teaching Skills	Student Readiness	Student Assessment
	◆ Organizational Strategies ◆ Controlling Participation ◆ Guide/Monitor ◆ Management of Student Behavior ◆ Computer and Media Skills ◆ Flexible	◆ Computer Skills ◆ Media Related Skills ◆ Highly Motivated ◆ Ability to Work in Groups ◆ Ability to Work Individually for Longer Periods of Time	◆ Group Presentations ◆ Individual Presentations ◆ Objective Tests ◆ Models ◆ Portfolios ◆ Multimedia Presentations

Case Method Plan for American History. The case method can be used in the block in two slightly differing ways. The first structure of a case involves the creation of a narrative which includes information or data about a specific subject area. After hearing the narrative or "case," students solve significant issues, research specified subject matter, or solve problems presented in the case. The students examine ideas of consequence, concepts, relevant issues and possibilities. The second structure for a case is the subject-centered method or individualized assignments, structured to explore a central subject. Both the narrative structure and the subject-centered approach to case method are effective ways of conducting student-driven study.

Subject-Centered Case Study - American History
Title: "High Seas Adventure"
Subject: Early Explorers - The Discovery of America

Day One: Introduce the need to explore and set the stage for exploration. Also as a part of this introduction, the teacher should present the case study of early explorers. Lecture in the introduction for approximately 15 minutes.

As a class, develop a **Web (Graphic Organizer)** of the Discovery of America. Allow students to recall as many explorers as they can remember from past social studies classes. Create a bulletin board or an entire wall in the classroom with their final web of explorers. After brainstorming, allow students to use their text to flesh out the web. Groups could be assigned to use their textbooks for additional information on a certain part of the web. These same groups will then take part in developing a bulletin board or wall graphic of the web. (See Example 2: Early Explorers Web.) The development of this web will take approximately 40–60 minutes of class time.

Assign individual topics in the web for students. The students will be responsible for discovering information related to early explorers through a specified subject. Each student should have a different topic. You may want to attach students' names to their topics on the web. The assigning of roles will take approximately 10 minutes.

EXAMPLE 2. EARLY EXPLORERS STUDENT-GENERATED WEB

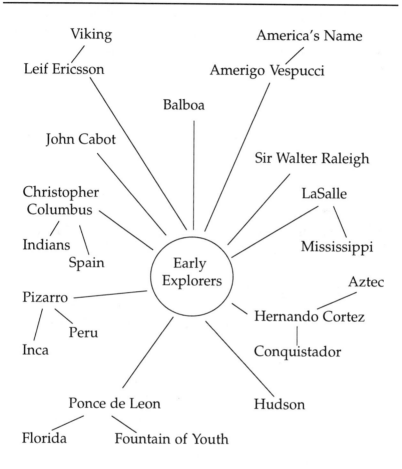

In the final 20 minutes of class refocus students on the initial lecture for the impetus of exploration. Give any additional background on the countries involved in exploration and discuss with students the relevance of these explorers to life in the United States today. The teacher may also use this time to have students read aloud from the textbook. For homework, students must read the chapter or section on exploration in their textbook and prepare to travel to the library on Day Two.

Day Two: Students travel to the library for research and individual conferences. During the library time, teachers can meet with each student to develop work contracts. (See Examples 3 and 4: Contract.) In the contract, the teacher and students agree on the type of individual projects which students can create from their research. This gives guidance and consistency to the case study.

Individual Projects

Possible individual case study projects could include any of the following examples and can be formally assigned or contracted with students for completion.

1. Three-dimensional or two-dimensional artwork: Sculpture, models, weavings, replications, inventions, drawings, or paintings are suitable for students who desire to communicate the major ideas or themes through the use of a visual media.

2. Multi-media: Power Point presentations, slide/sound shows, HyperCard or other hypermedia programs, video presentations, or the development of artwork, plans, caricatures, newspaper accounts, and information packets with computers can reinforce writing and technology skills.

3. Literary: Books, newspapers, magazines, journals, narratives, biographies, plays, scripts, and fictional stories are an excellent means to record research material. Interviews: Gathering information from personal accounts, anecdotes, oral histories, recollections, can enhance understanding of events, eras, and issues.

4. Scientific Experiments: Designing and carrying out credible, reliable, controlled experiments that involve practice with formulating hypotheses, predicting, data collection, data recording, interpreting, and drawing a conclusion help develop students' problem-solving abilities.

EXAMPLE 3: CONTRACT

STUDENT CASE STUDY CONTRACT

Student Name:_____ Period:_____

Case Study Title:_____

Please describe in one paragraph your proposal for an individual or group project. You will be responsible for integrating your project into the case solution. Will anyone be working with you and if so, what will their role be in the research and presentation?

Develop a timeline for your project. Include the starting date, research time, project development time, and final presentation day.

Starting Date:_____

Presentation Date:_____

My goals during the case study include:

1 -

2 -

3 -

I hereby agree to this learning contract and to the responsibilities of presentation in solving the case entitled
_____.

_____   _____
Student Signature   Teacher Signature

EXAMPLE 4: CONTRACT

PROJECT CONTRACT

Student Name:_____   Class Period:_____

For my project, I plan to...

_____ I will NOT work with a partner.

_____ I will work with a partner.

My responsibilities for this project include:

My partner's responsibilities for this project include:

Rough Draft of Written Assignment Due:_____

Individual Conference Scheduled For:_____

Presentation Due:_____

By signing this contract I agree to meet all deadlines and produce a project which is original and appropriate for the assignment. I further agree to give my best effort on this project.

_____
                    Student Signature

PROJECT GRADE:_____

Teacher Comments:

5. Music: Creating and/or interpreting music and lyrics that reflect the values and the political and social climate of a period can also help students gain insight into past events.

Student Presentations

Presentations during a case study are essential to share knowledge gained by each student and to "solve" the case. Presentations may be the result of group research or individual activities. Examples of possible student presentations include:

1. *Theater:* Plays, poetry readings, readers theater, monologues of literary works, presentations of original one-act plays creatively allow students to present findings.

2. *Simulations and Debates:* Students can participate in simulations at a safe distance while practicing skills of analysis, interpretation, and presentation. Simulations and debates allow the students to explore complex and often controversial legal and social issues in a protected environment. Both the participating students and those who observe the simulation or debates work beyond the comprehension level, the material is internalized.

3. *Fashion Shows and Festivals:* Using clothing, food, music, and visual props to portray trends and changes in social values of specific periods enable students to gain first-hand knowledge of a person, place, or time.

4. *Oral Presentations:* Oral presentations reflect students' research, comprehension, and analysis of a particular topic of study. Oral presentations are an excellent means to communicate large amounts of information in a short period of time.

5. *Written Presentations:* Formal assignments may be given to students on a contractual topic related to a case study. This is often done in conjunction with a performance part to the presentation. Written assignments require outside research, interviews, and data gathering to provide a strong basis for understanding. Possible assignments could include research reports, scrapbooks, manuals, annotated bibliographies, editorials, journals, biographies, scenarios, and critiques.

Special Projects

Field studies or special projects require active involvement of students in applying the general principles of classroom learning to real-life situations. Moving knowledge beyond the classroom walls can be a benefit of the case study. These special projects may last for one day or for an entire semester. Examples of field studies may include:

1. *Community Service:* Working with social service agencies and in community programs such as a soup kitchen, a recycling center, a fish hatchery, a wildlife refuge, a preservation society for heritage/historical buildings, an after-school program for homeless children, a children's hospital, and homes for the elderly.

2. *Work Experience and Volunteer Work:* Participating in jobs in the community to gain firsthand work experience.

3. *Surveys:* Collecting and analyzing data related to issues of community, civic, or national concern.

4. *Cultural Exchanges:* Participating with students from culturally diverse areas. Exchange programs may involve travel, the exchange of videos or letters to pen pals.

5. *Field Trips:* Making direct investigations in the field moves students beyond simulations.

6. **Community Study:** Examining various components of a working community help students to understand the social, political, and economic forces at work.

7. **Adventure:** Challenging students to take hiking expeditions, develop physical skill, undertake Outward Bound trips, ropes courses, or other new appropriate experiences.

Day Three: Lecture on maritime sailing and the conditions our first settlers endured aboard ship. This lecture should last for approximately 10 minutes and include the reading of first-person narratives from slaves, explorers and young travelers.

Transition should be made from the travel to the new world to a map study of the new world itself. Distribute topographical maps of North America to students and have them refer to the map section of their textbook. Students will lead an expedition across the United States and must develop a plan to submit to the pioneers. Students will also visit a large map located at the front of the room to draw their individual case study explorer's route from Europe to the New World. Students will do this with markers the teacher provides. After tracing these routes, discuss the overhead map of European ownership of the new world. This discussion should last 20 minutes as students will take notes and read sections of the textbook that apply to the division of the new world. Finally, the last 10 minutes of class will be used to review the case study and expectations for the student presentations. Presentations will be given on Days Four and Five of the case study.

Day Four: Student presentations of their case study should be made just prior to the concluding activity. During the student presentations, students will complete an evaluation slip for each presenter and take notes on the information. (See Example 5: Student-Peer Evaluation.) The students are responsible for all information and must eventually write an essay on exploration comparing the motivation, journey, lands explored, people encountered, and the results of at least four explorers. The explorers must be sponsored by different countries. Stu-

EXAMPLE 5. STUDENT-PEER EVALUATION

STUDENT - PEER EVALUATION SLIP

Name of Evaluator:_____

Name of Presenter:_____

Topic:_____

I most enjoyed . . .

I did not understand . . .

Rank the overall effectiveness of the presentation.
1= Excellent to 5 = Needs Improvement

1   2   3   4   5

List one interesting fact you learned from this speaker.

dents will use the individual presentations to write this essay. Students will also participate in a Socratic seminar tomorrow (Day Five) and will discuss all explorers.

Day Five: A Socratic seminar on Day Five will enable students to debrief the entire case. After all individual presentations have been made, students participate in a seminar as the culmination of all case study activities. To begin the seminar, students will be instructed to develop five questions about the explorers. Students will also write a list of reasons they believe a person would travel through unknown waters to distant lands. Students sit in a circle and are instructed to discover an answer to the following set of questions:

1. What caused explorers to make perilous journeys to the new world?

2. What would our country be like today if we had initially been ruled by Spain, France, or Portugal?

3. Which explorer was the most influential? Why?

4. Which explorer was the most ruthless? Why?

5. What was the most significant discovery made by the explorers?

6. How do these past explorations affect us today?

As the students respond, ask questions and develop answers to the set of questions, the teacher will score participation on the Seminar Rubric. Grades will be determined based on the number and quality of questions posed and answers given. (See Examples 6 and 7: Seminar Rubric and the Marked Example.)

Cooperative Learning For Biology. Various models of cooperative learning will be highly effective in the block schedule if they are used correctly. If cooperative learning activities use heterogeneous teams, have teammate interdependence and individual accountability, they should enable students to actively participate in the learning process. When teams are heterogeneously grouped, a cross section of all ability levels may be found in each group. To ensure teammate interdependence, students must be taught a series of group expectations and the meaning of group work. When each student is accountable for completing his or her own portion of the work, teammate interdependence is possible. Students must realize that they cannot complete the activity without one another. Many teachers will assign roles of various natures to help promote interdependence and accountability. These roles often include leader, scribe, recorder, monitor, supporter, materials expert, etc. Successful group activities stem from a well-developed classroom management plan for grouping. The plan should include procedures for contribution, determining tasks, checking for accuracy or completion, keeping on task, and evaluating the final product.

We have found the most successful group organization to be the Jigsaw II, which involves an expert group and a peer

EXAMPLE 6. SEMINAR RUBRIC

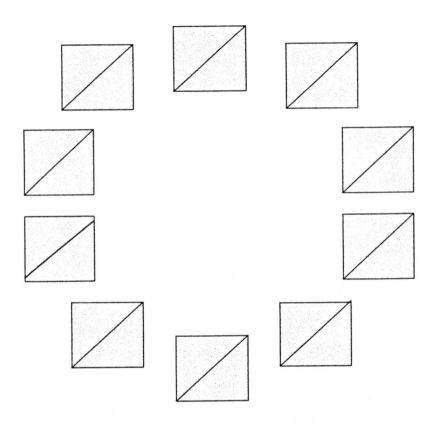

Top Portion of Box = Number of Questions Asked by the Student

Bottom Portion of Box = Number of Answers Given by the Student

** Write each student's name next to a box and record with
hash marks as each student participates in the seminar.

Example 7. Seminar Rubric - Marked Example

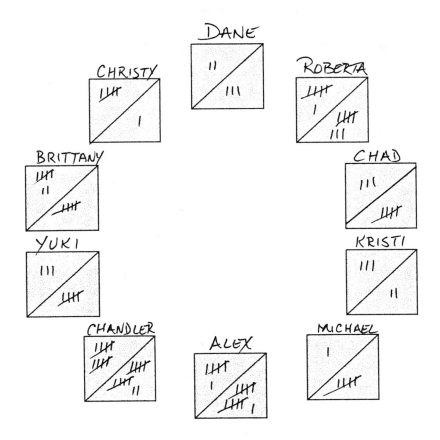

training group. Each student is responsible for attaining a set amount of information in the expert group and then move to a second group to teach this information to other students. The following is an example of **Jigsaw II** in a biology class.

Jigsaw II - Article Share - Vocabulary Building Activity
Open the class with a 15-minute lecture on genetic engineering and the implications to students' lives. Introduce the Jigsaw II movement patterns and the responsibilities of each student in the process. Assign students to one of the following expert groups:

Group One - Genetic Engineering in Agriculture
Transgenic Animals, Plants, Pesticides
Group Two: Genetic Fingerprinting
Criminal Justice, Archaeology
Group Three: Genetic Engineering in Medicine
Inherited Diseases, Gene Therapy
Group Four: Economics of Genetic Research
Pesticides, Agriculture, Animal Rights

For approximately 30 minutes, students read their assigned group articles, take notes to share with other groups, and create a list of 10 vocabulary words and definitions from the articles. The list of vocabulary words and the definitions should be written on an overhead sheet to be shared with the whole class after the grouping activity. From the expert groups, students move to predetermined peer sharing groups that should be comprised of a student each from groups 1, 2, 3, and 4. Each student will share notes and all vocabulary terms for 25 minutes.

After students have had the opportunity to present their expert group information, the teacher will lead a short class discussion to determine if each group successfully taught their assigned information. This class discussion will take approximately 15 minutes and will also include a quiz. Allow students to use their notes during the quiz. Students who participated and learned from all expert group representatives will do well on the quiz. During the final 5 minutes of class, the teacher should review each group topic and assign textbook reading on genetic engineering for homework. (See visual representation of Jigsaw II in Example 8.)

EXAMPLE 8. VISUAL REPRESENTATION OF JIGSAW II - COOPERATIVE LEARNING LESSON

(15 Min.)	Lecture on genetic engineering Assign expert groups
(30 Min.)	Expert groups meet to become experts on reading material Students record 10 vocabulary terms and definitions
(25 Min.)	Peer groups meet and each student presents material from his or her expert group Each student records information from other expert group representatives
(15 Min.)	Teacher leads short discussion of group experiences Quiz given to students - class notes may be used
(5 Min.)	Homework assignment Review of each genetic engineering topic

Integrated Unit for Psychology or Journalism.

Day One: The Media and Society

A. Introduction to Mass Media and Their Influence on Society
B. What Makes Us Vulnerable to Persuasion?
C. How Does Persuasion Work?

Activity Prior to Introduction:
Ad Count - Students count the number of times they encounter any kind of advertisement during the course of one day. On the first day of the unit, students will average their counts and multiply the average by 365 days.

Ongoing Unit Activity:
Scrapbook - Students will create a scrapbook in which they keep at least 15 examples of magazine ads or descriptions of television and radio ads. Under each example, students will describe how the ad illustrates the principles studied in class.

Day Two: Information and Influence - The Use and Misuse of Information

A. Principles
    1. The Misuse of Random and Ambiguous Data
    2. The Sleeper Effect
    3. Indirect Influence
B. Applications
    1. Emotional Evidence (The use of anecdotes and appeals)
    2. Rational Evidence (Misread and out-of-context data)
C. Quiz #1

Group Activity:
The Consumer Challenge—Provide student groups with

magazines, newspapers, and selected taped commercials. Have students list the outlandish claims and "evidence" used to sell products. From this list, groups will select a company to call for substantiation of these claims. During a political election, tape political ads and list the claims made by each candidate. Write to these politicians and ask for substantiation of these claims.

Daily Activity:

Appeals to Reason vs. Emotion—Show students a sample of an emotional appeal and a rational appeal. Have students compose their own appeal by rewriting the emotional appeal as a rational appeal and vice versa.

Day Three: Exposure and Influence—The Media and Culture

A. Principles

1. Weak Messages

2. Repetition

B. Applications

1. Covert Messages, Norms and Socialization in the Media

2. Status, Roles, and Stereotypes in the Media Review

Group Activity: (Jigsaw II)

Media and Culture—Students meet with their expert group to read articles, examine samples and discuss the ways in which the media define our ideas of people. Expert group topics include racial or gender representation, racial stereotypes, sex-roles, representations of religion, and symbols of status. During the second round each "expert" shares his or her ideas with a peer group.

Class Activity:

Compare Magazines—Students compare two magazines that are targeted for a similar audience. Record all student ideas about the type of reader who would purchase each magazine and then test these assumptions. To test the assumptions, students will graph the number of times appeals are made to any of the following: the need for reassurance of value, the need for ego boosting, the need for emotional stability, the need to be creative, the need to love someone, the need to be loved, the need to collect or obtain objects, the need for power, and the need for identity.

Day Four: Communication and Influence - Techniques of Persuasion

    A. Principles

        1. Influence Through Commitment

        2. Faulty Reasoning Designed to Persuade

    B. Applications

        1. Foot-in-the-Door Phenomenon

        2. Faulty Reasoning and Other Devices of Propaganda

Class Activity:
Propaganda Film Analysis—Students identify the propaganda techniques used in a Nazi propaganda film and a U.S. Cold War newsreel. Students discuss the control of news during the Gulf War. Students will finally develop poster-size charts delineating the pros and cons of government control of the media during war and peace.

Class Activity:
Presidential Debate—Students watch a previous debate and analyze the arguments for evidence of faulty reasoning. Students should suggest/predict alternative arguments or retorts. Stop the video periodically and ask students to evaluate the reasoning of the candidates and possible alternative responses.

Day Five: Wrap-Up

    A. Identifying Cues

        1. Verbal Cues (Repetition and Intonation)

        2. Non-verbal Cues (Body Language)

        3. Internal Cues (Sensing Conformity Pressure)

    B. Culminating Activity: Projects and Open House

Reinforcement Activity:

Nonverbal Persuasion—Show the students a series of television ads with the sound turned off. Have them identify the principles of persuasion in body language, facial expression, and camera maneuvers.

Verbal Persuasion—To remind students that there are positive uses for persuasion, have them listen to Dr. Martin Luther King's "I Have a Dream" speech, or John F. Kennedy's inaugural address. Students should identify verbal cues of persuasion.

Culminating Activity:

Scrapbook—Each student will select four pages from his or her scrapbook to present as the best samples. These student pages should be displayed in collage form on one the classroom walls.

Ad Skits—In groups, students should design an ad for a political campaign. The ad should illustrate four principles of persuasion and will be performed on the following class day.

The suggestions that follow were assembled during 4x4 seminars throughout the United States over the course of the past three years.

Instructional Ideas

♦ Less lecturing

♦ More group activities

♦ Working for creativity

♦ Coordinated instruction between disciplines - units

♦ Seminar method

♦ Guest lecturers - community involvement

♦ More multimedia

♦ Labs using practical hands-on approach

♦ Individualize - address learning styles

♦ Problem solving

♦ Case studies

♦ Leave school building - Leave for only one period - teleconferencing

- Simulated learning
- Time for writing in journals
- Time for more one-on-one instruction
- Teacher facilitator - students have more responsibility
- Time for remediation
- Show correlation to careers - site visits and placements in the community
- Hands-on approach to teaching

Suggestions for Success

- Commitment and cooperation of all faculty
- Educational input from the community
- Preplanning - research, workshops, visitation to other programs
- Administrative understanding and support
- Parent and student understanding and support
- Entire school should be on the same schedule
- Ongoing evaluations - modifications and changes as needed
- Open spaces - facilities conducive to activities offered
- Positive attitudes
- High expectations
- Share ideas between departments, teams, and administration
- Communication between faculty and administration
- More teacher assistants
- Increase in teacher assistance programs - support staff
- Full financial support
- Consider weaknesses - have ideas and plans to combat
- Increase supply budget by 25 percent

Instructional Evaluation

Instructional evaluation, or assessment, was once exclusively the teacher's domain. It consisted mainly of predetermined paper and pencil testing. Periodically, the students would read a book, write a report, and give an oral presentation, activities which would all have to live up to the expectations of the individual teacher. Now assessment is not necessarily based upon the sole; personal judgment of the teacher. Students are included. As the community demands more student accountability, students are becoming more involved in their own learning process.

Instructional evaluation occurs through the assessment of student achievement. Instruction is evaluated by the effectiveness of the instructor. For example, does the teacher choose the right delivery system? Are the teacher's objectives clear? Do test items relate to objectives? Evaluation of instruction is also evaluation of the curriculum. It reveals the success of one dimension. How much the student achieves in areas that are assessed. It may also indicate whether the content has been adequately covered. Evaluation of instruction does not answer curricular concerns as to whether the subject matter was the right choice, whether its content is relevant, whether it meets student or societal needs, and whether it has been selected wisely.

Methods of Instructional Evaluation

Measurement is the means of determining the degrees of achievement of a particular competency. Testing is the use of instruments for measuring achievement. The three phases of instructional evaluation are *preassessment, formative evaluation,* and *summative evaluation.* Evaluation that takes place before instruction is called preassessment. Evaluation that takes place during the instruction process is called formative evaluation. Assessment that takes place at the end of instruction is called summative evaluation.

Preassessment. The tool used in preassessment is the criterion-referenced test or pretest. The criterion-referenced test measures the entry skills that have been identified to be critical to beginning instruction. There are several ways that criterion-referenced tests can be used:

♦ for preassessment

♦ for formative testing,

♦ to determine whether components of the instructional model need modification, and

♦ to determine whether students have achieved the criterion levels of objectives.

The pretest is criterion-referenced to the objectives the designer intends to teach. A pretest by itself is not sufficient to address all needs at the beginning of instruction. If students perform poorly on a pretest, the instructor may not be able to gauge whether they did poorly for lack of general knowledge or specifically the knowledge required for entry level instruction.

A second type of test is designed to help students measure their skills against the skills of others. These types of tests are called norm-referenced tests. Norm-referenced measurement compares a student's performance on a test to the performance of other students who took the test. Norm-referenced testing is necessary when a limited number of spaces are to be filled from a pool of applicants. Norm-referenced measurement permits comparisons among people, with the primary purpose of making decisions about the qualifications of individuals.

Formative Evaluation. Formative evaluation consists of formal and informal techniques of assessing the learning of students. Formative evaluation occurs during the process of instruction. It may include questions at different points during the instruction or checking students' responses to parts of the instruction. Instructors use formative evaluation to determine if the skills to be learned are being addressed. It allows instructors to determine whether they need to provide remedial instruction to overcome difficulties.

Summative Evaluation. Summative evaluation is the assessment that occurs at the end of a course or unit. The tools used are final exams, a post-test, or an actual demonstration of a skill or operation. It is used to determine whether students have mastered the instruction.

Assessment of Student Achievement. Several new ways are available to evaluate student achievement. The new tools are called performance-based or authentic assessment. Authentic means "worthy of acceptance or belief, trustworthy" (Engel, 1994, p.24). Assessments are authentic because they are valuable activities within themselves and involve the performance of tasks that are directly related to real-world problems.

Portfolios, authentic assessment measures, and alternative assessment activities are the latest buzzwords used to describe activities other than standardized tools for determining a student's achievement. Educators, parents, and students have come to realize that standardized tests do not truly represent a student's growth in the content knowledge, skills, and the instructional activities in the classroom.

Some of these buzzwords follow:

♦ Assessment: an exercise such as a written test, portfolio, or experiment that seeks to measure a student's knowledge in a subject area.

♦ Portfolio: a systematic and organized collection of a student's work throughout a course or school year which measures the student's knowledge and skills and often includes some form of self-reflection by the student.

♦ Alternative assessment: any form of measuring what a student knows and is able to do other than traditional standardized tests. Alternative forms of assessment include portfolios, performance-based assessments, and other means of testing students. These alternative assessments show actual growth over a period of time that the students, parents, and teachers can physically see. Tests do not show this growth occurring.

♦ Authentic assessment: allowing the student to "become progressively self-disciplined as a thinker . . .

(and) to acquire the habit of inquiring and engaging in discourse with care and thoroughness" (Wiggins, 1993). Its purpose is to get students to take control of their own learning while maintaining relevance and a meaningful connection to what they are learning. Student contracts enable students to take responsibility for their own learning while giving them freedom to explore and teaches organizational control of the lesson content.

PORTFOLIO

The portfolio is the most popular form of alternative assessment and is authentic assessment when done correctly. A portfolio is a collection of student writing samples assembled over a period of a course or longer. It is like a collection of photographs of a student's writing. When analyzing each writing sample singularly, a complete picture cannot be attained. The portfolio allows for a comprehensive evaluation of a student's growth and the creation of individual goals for future work.

A portfolio is called a performance-based assessment because the intent of the portfolio is for students to assemble a collection of samples of their work, which in essence shows evidence of their accomplishments. Portfolios may contain creative writing, tests, artwork, exercises, reflective essays, notes on topics, and whatever other materials portray achievement. Standards and criteria for achievement in portfolios should be set. Some of the criteria may include completeness, effort, neatness, and creativity. Portfolios reveal students and allow teachers and students to work in the most productive ways possible. There are almost as many approaches to compiling and evaluating portfolios as there are proponents of this form of assessment. Portfolios can be used both formally and informally. Ideally, the portfolio captures the evolution of the student's ideas and can be used instructionally and as progress markers for the student, teacher, and program evaluator.

Portfolios are adaptable to a variety of educational settings. In Fort Worth, Texas, a fifth grade teacher used them in his math class. Kentucky and Vermont educators have made portfolios a part of their statewide assessment of students. Pittsburgh educators have used portfolios to assess learning in imaginative writing, music, and visual arts.

A portfolio has three major parts: biography, range of works, and reflections. The biography shows the developmental history of the child's progress and gives the reader an impression of how the student has progressed from the beginning to that point. The portfolio contains a variety of assignments. These could be the student's "best," "most important," "satisfactory," and "unsatisfactory" pieces of work as well as revisions. The student critiques his or her work by reflecting on how his or her performance has changed, what he or she has learned, and what he or she needs to do in order to improve. (See Example 8: Portfolio Models.)

Educators who use portfolios in the 4x4 block believe that these are practical and effective assessment tools for several reasons. Portfolios are easy to design, durable, and reusable. This form of assessment impacts the teacher's way of teaching and testing by problem solving, communication, application, etc., and promotes worthwhile learning while expanding the dimensions of education. It provides a developmental perspective that is easily observed by students, parents, and teachers. Finally, it documents a student's progress through school until graduation. Members of the NEA support the portfolio's use because it accurately reflects what the student has learned.

Not all educators support the portfolio. Some teachers use it to display the best of a student's work. Under this condition, it will not accurately reflect performance and rate of progress and cannot be called an assessment measure because, rather than including a representative sampling of a student's work, teachers may guide students as to what to write and include. Storage is difficult because a portfolio, if used appropriately, can be big and bulky. Scoring is time-consuming as well as inconsistent, and even if the scorers do agree, that does not guarantee that the portfolio measures what it was supposed to measure (Viadero, 1995). In Vermont it took more than 160 scorers five days to assess 7,000 portfolios. These scorers were, understandably, influenced by their personal beliefs.

EXAMPLE 8. PORTFOLIO MODELS

Model #1

I. Introduction - Title Page

II. Student Portrait - Photo or Video Montage of Student

    A. Attendance Record

    B. Discipline Record

    C. Self-esteem Rating

    D. Test Scores

III. Educational Goals

    A. Student Goals for the Year

    B. Career Goals

    C. Copies of Exceptional Work - All Discipline Areas

IV. Conclusion - Reflection

    A. Evaluation of Portfolio

    B. Summary Paper at End of Year - Student Self-Evaluation

EXAMPLE 8. PORTFOLIO MODELS, CONTINUED

Model #2

I. Writing

   A. Submissions from English: Literature Response, Personal Essay, Research Paper

   B. Submissions from History: Cause-and-Effect Paper, Defense Paper

   C. Submissions from Science: Classification Paper, Lab Report

   D. Submission of Student Choice

II. Reading List

III. Conclusion

   A. Self-Evaluation of Writing and Reading Goals

   B. Teacher Analysis of Writing Ability - Establish Goals for Next School Year

EXAMPLE 8. PORTFOLIO MODELS, CONTINUED

Model #3

I. Student Goals for the School Year
   A. Writing Goals
   B. Reading Goals
   C. Communication Goals

II. Writing Samples
   A. Literature Response
   B. Comparative Analysis
   C. Journal Entry
   D. Research Paper
   E. Essay Test
   F. Creative Writing - Poem, Short Story, etc.
   G. Student Choice

III. Editing
   A. Peer Evaluation
   B. Self-Evaluation

IV. Future Goals for Writing and Reading
   A. List of Future Goals
   B. Summary of Career Goals

Teachers participating in 4x4 seminars expressed the following suggestions for evaluation success:

Assessment and Evaluation

♦ Reports

♦ Team competitions, research projects

♦ Skills

♦ Role-playing

♦ Portfolios

♦ More oral response time, debates

♦ Team projects

♦ Self-assessment

♦ Individual

♦ Pre- and post-tests

♦ Teacher-student evaluation, one-on-one

♦ Practical hands-on skill evaluation, theory into practice

♦ Peer evaluations

♦ Standardized testing

♦ Parent conferences

♦ Ongoing evaluation of program, formative evaluation

♦ More home involvement

♦ Non-threatening evaluations for teachers, opportunities to try things without fear of failure or accountability

UNIT EVALUATION

Unit evaluation includes two major types of evaluation: diagnostic and summative. Diagnostic evaluation allows the teacher to learn what the students' learning potential is prior to the start of the instruction. Summative evaluation measures what the students have learned through implementation of the unit.

The usual form of evaluation is a written test. The unit test can contain a mix of objective (answer with the facts) and subjective (essay) questions. These two types of evaluation assist with the planning of future methods of teaching a unit by providing, through student response to test items, information about how the instruction can be organized to become more effective.

LESSON EVALUATION

Lesson evaluation occurs daily. Informal and formal evaluation occurs while the lesson is going on as well as upon its completion. Some informal ways of evaluation are observations of the students individually and as a group, assessment of students' contributions, review of homework, and overall impressions of the level of student understanding and success. Some formal ways of evaluation are quizzes, debates, and rating scales. These evaluations are done constantly throughout the lesson to verify that the lesson is being comprehended by the students. They allow for modifications to be made at any point in the lesson.

MAINTAINING A POSITIVE CLASSROOM CLIMATE THROUGH INSTRUCTION

Students and teachers learning in a 4x4 model of block scheduling become more active and engage in hands-on activities. The classroom climate is positively affected by this active learning. During the lengthened class period, students and teachers have the opportunity to get to know one another better. Teachers have fewer students in one day and spend longer periods of time with individual students. This one-on-one time helps to build strong relationships between students and teachers.

To improve the classroom climate, a strong management program is important. The classroom management program puts boundaries and limits on student behavior and gives opportunities for the students to learn in a safe environment. Along with more engaging and hands-on learning, students benefit from a warm and inviting environment. The classroom climate will improve if teachers can create learning activities that are student-friendly, have a positive attitude, be approachable, and decorate the classroom in a pleasing and educational manner. The school building itself can also be a warm and nurturing place. Bulletin boards that clearly display upcoming events, lists of students with perfect attendance, lists of awards and honors, honor roll lists and athletic achievements are both visually interesting and communicative. Giant calendars, club-sponsored bulletin boards, and festive holiday decorations make the school more personal and aid in creating a positive learning environment.

REFERENCES

Couch, R. (1993). *Synectics and imagery: Developing creative thinking through images.*

Ennis, Robert H. (1993, Summer). *Critical Thinking Assessment: Theory Into Practice*, pp. 179–186.

Frasier, Chapman Hood. (1997, January). *The Development of an Authentic Assessment Instrument:The Scored Discussion. The English Journal*, pp. 37–40.

Joyce, B. & Weil, M. (1996). *Models of Teaching.* Englewood Cliffs, New Jersey: Prentice-Hall..

Lewis, A. & Smith, D. (1993, Summer). *Defining Higher Order Thinking. Theory Into Practice.* pp. 40–48.

McBumey, Donald H. (1995, February). *The Problem Method of Teaching Research Methods: Teaching Psychology M*, pp.36–38.

Parsons, J. & Smith, D. (1993). *Valuing, Students: Rethinking Evaluation.* ERIC Document Reproduction Service No. ED 362 304).

Pike, K.& Salend, S.J. (1995, Fall*). Authentic Assessment Strategies: Alternatives to Norm-Referenced Testing. Teaching Exceptional Children.* pp. 15–20.

Silver, Harvey F., Strong, Richard W., & Hanson, J. Robert. (1988). *Teaching strategies library.* Association for Supervision and Curriculum Development, Alexandria, VA.

Sudzina, Mary R. (1993, February). *Dealing with Diversity Issues in the Classroom: A Case Study Approach.* Paper presented at the annual meeting of the Association of Teacher

Educators, Los Angeles. (ERIC Document Reproduction Service No. ED 354 233).